FORMED
BY THE
DESERT

Copyright © 1997 and 2000 Joyce Huggett (Text only)
        © 1996 Jon Arnold (Photographs only)

This edition published 2000

The rights of Joyce Huggett to be identified as author of this work has been asserted by her in accordance with the Copyright, Design and Patents Act 1988.

Published by Eagle, an imprint of Inter Publishing Service (IPS) Ltd, PO Box 530, Guildford, Surrey GU2 4FH.

British Library Cataloguing in Publication Data. A catalogue record for this book is available from the British Library.

Scripture quotations unless otherwise stated are taken from the Holy Bible, New International Version. Copyright © 1973, 1978, 1984 by the International Bible Society. Used by permission of Hodder & Stoughton, a Division of Hodder Headline. GNB: Good News Bible; JB: J.B. Phillips; LB: Living Bible.

Typeset by Eagle Publishing
Printed by Gutenberg Press Limited, Malta
ISBN No: 0 86347 396 2

FORMED BY THE DESERT

Heart-to-heart Encounters with God

Joyce Huggett

Photographs by

Jon Arnold

eagle

Guildford, Surrey

For
JM

With warm thanks for accompanying me
through the long desert of transition

Contents

Rainbow over acacia tree, near the Dead Sea

Introduction

The Spirit of God, like a giant kite, hovers over an empty, dark void – that's what we see when the curtain rises on Genesis 1:

> Now the earth was formless and empty,
> darkness was over the surface of the deep,
> and the Spirit of God was hovering over the waters.
>
> (Genesis 1:2)

Jesus, promising to return to take us to his holy city; Jesus offering the free gift of living water to the thirsty – that's what we see as the curtain falls on Revelation 22:

> The Spirit and the bride say, 'Come!'
> Whoever is thirsty, let him come;
> and whoever wishes, let him take the free gift
> of the water of life – that flows through the city.[1]

Sandwiched between the garden the Spirit planted in the world he created and the city whose main street is awash with life-giving water lies an enormous stretch of desert.[2] Some of the finest stalwarts of the faith were shaped by this desert – people like Abraham and Sarah, Moses and Miriam, Elijah, Hosea and his wife, Gomer, the psalmists, John the Baptist – and Jesus himself.

Inspired by these spiritual giants who spent so much time wandering in the wilderness, Christian pilgrims down the ages have wended their way to places like the Sinai peninsular, the Judaean desert and present-day Jordan, the Arabian desert of the Bible writers. I, too, have spent a certain amount of time in

the physical desert – savouring its silence, listening to its
language, observing desert dwellers. In fact, making a pilgrimage
in the desert on one occasion made a profound impact on me.
Here I found God speaking in an unforgettable, over-powering
way. He spoke, not to my head only but, more significantly, to
my heart – gently increasing my self-awareness and in that way
showing me attitudes that needed to change and be changed. He
also demonstrated how essential and deliciously liberating it is
to trust him and revealed how patient and tender he is. Here,
too, he filled my heart with awe as I gazed at the sunset and the
moon rise, as I lay under the vast, star-studded canopy we call
heaven and as I sat on a sun-scorched rock scarcely daring to
breathe lest I should shatter the all-enveloping silence. Best of all,
he gave me a renewed, felt closeness to Jesus, the Lord of the
Desert with whom this book starts.

I had read books written by desert dwellers but no book can
really prepare the pilgrim for their first encounter with the
dazzling desert. Desert terrain leaves us shell-shocked, awed,
humbled, changed, aware of God's greatness and our own
littleness, God's worth-ship and our own insignificance. We find
sentiments expressed by the psalmist echoing round the
labyrinths of our being:

I look up at your macro-skies, dark and enormous,
your hand-made jewelry,
Moon and stars mounted in their settings.
Then I look at my micro-self and wonder,
Why do you bother with us?
Why take a second look our way?

(Psalm 8:1,4)[3]

If I read the signs of the times correctly, countless Christians
today yearn for a heart-to-heart encounter with God. In the

mystery of who he is, God woos such people away from the props and luxuries that camouflage need and conceal desire and he *lures* them into the desert. The word *lure* is a powerful one. Among other things, it describes the method falconers use to recall their trainee hawks. Attaching a bunch of feathers to a cord and hiding the hawk's food inside them, the falconer entices the bird back home. The word *lure*, when used by God, has warm, tender, even passionate overtones. So he says of Hosea's wife, Gomer:

> 'I am going to lure her
> and lead her out into the wilderness
> and speak to her heart.
> I am going to give her back her vineyards . . .
> There she will respond to me as she did when she was young.'
>
> (Hosea 2:14 JB)

We are not all drawn into the *physical* desert by God – neither can we all travel to Sinai or Syria, Jordan or Egypt. We may well encounter desert-like periods of our life, however. As this revised edition of the book goes to print, my prayer is that readers may shed the commonly-held belief that if they are in a place of emotional or spiritual dryness, they must have *failed* God in some way. Instead, I pray that the questions with which some of the chapters end may help them assess whether there may be more positive reasons why the landscape of their heart resembles the wilderness wastes that are so wonderfully captured in the photographs with which this book is illustrated; that they may be open to the possibility that God has wooed them into the desert to draw them closer to himself.

Joyce Huggett

Sunrise in the Sinai range

Two Desert Songs

The heavens declare the glory of God;
   the skies proclaim the work of his hands.
Day after day they pour forth speech;
   night after night they display knowledge.
There is no speech or language
   where their voice is not heard.
Their voice goes out into all the earth,
   their words to the ends of the world.

In the heavens he has pitched a tent for the sun,
   which is like a bridegroom coming forth from his pavilion,
   like a champion rejoicing to run his course.
It rises at one end of the heavens
   and makes its circuit to the other;
   nothing is hidden from its heat.

                             (Psalm 19:1–6)

By the word of the Lord were the heavens made,
   their starry host by the breath of his mouth.
He gathers the waters of the sea into jars;
   he puts the deep into storehouses.
Let all the earth fear the LORD;
   let all the people of the world revere him.
For he spoke, and it came to be;
   he commanded, and it stood firm.

                             (Psalm 33:6–9)

ONE

Jesus

Lord of the Desert

Many milestones mark Jesus' transition from a foetus to a man: his memorable birth, for example, his refugee status in Egypt, his first visit to the Temple in Jerusalem and his testing in the wilderness.

Mark sums up the latter in a nutshell:

> Jesus came from Nazareth in Galilee and was baptised by John in the Jordan. The moment he came out of the water, he saw the sky split open and God's Spirit, looking like a dove, come down on him. Along with the Spirit, a voice: 'You are my Son, chosen and marked by my love, pride of my life.' At once, this same Spirit pushed Jesus out into the wild. For forty wilderness days and nights he was tested by Satan. Wild animals were his companions, and angels took care of him.
>
> (Mark 1:9–12)[1]

Jesus' desert contest with Satan is played out against a particular background. Let's put the contest in context.

For thirty years, Jesus has lived in obscurity. His relationship with his Father has deepened (Luke 2:52). He has grown aware that he possesses exceptional powers.[2] He has realised that, one day, when the time is ripe, he must leave Nazareth. Like a tracker dog picking up a scent, instinct tells him that his cousin's emergence from the desert is his cue. Bidding farewell to his home, he journeys to the Jordan where he witnesses the God-hungry crowds that are flocking to listen to this cousin, John the Baptist.

Wishing to identify himself with the resurgence of the desire for God that is taking the nation by storm, Jesus descends into the waters of baptism. Rising from the Jordan, he prays. While he's still at prayer, God wings never-to be-forgotten words right into his heart: 'You are my Son, whom I love; with you I am well pleased' (Mark 1:11).

'You are my Son . . .' Jesus knows that there's more to this affirmation than first meets the eye. It really means, 'You are my Messiah', for, throbbing through that simple statement Jesus hears a faint echo from one of the psalms that describes the Messiah: 'He said to me, "You are my Son; today I have become your Father" ' (Psalm 2:7).

'With you I am well pleased . . .' This phrase, too, conceals a hidden message. It, too, resonates with a prophecy from the past that now rings in Jesus' ears: 'Here is my servant, whom I uphold, my chosen one in whom I delight' (Isaiah 42:1).

This 'Servant passage', Jesus knows, culminates in the Suffering Servant picture Isaiah paints in chapter 53. Jesus registers the cost just as he registers the confirmation of his Messianic call.

'Whom I love . . .' Here there are no innuendos – just pure, affirming, expressed love – a love that does not embrace Jesus for what he does (his public ministry has not yet begun); but a love that enfolds him simply because he is.

He ascends Jordan's banks with a mandate: to fulfil his costly Messianic role – to usher in God's Kingdom.

He is surrounded by hundreds of people whose hearts are wide open to welcome Kingdom seed. He thrills to the sight. The crowd is ready. He's ready. Surely the moment for his Messianic ministry has come? Isn't this the moment he's been waiting for?

But no. God's Spirit does not open his lips and permit him to preach or teach. Instead, the Spirit silences him and drives him into the desert. The Spirit knows that, before a person acts, they need time and space to listen. The Spirit knows that, at the outset of his ministry, this is a lesson Jesus must learn.

Is he reluctant to go? Is that why Mark uses that forceful, colourful word *ekballo* that means to thrust away, even to expel him to the desert? Possibly.[3] Yet Jesus obeys. He exchanges the eager faces, hungry eyes and clamouring questions of the crowd for a new set of companions: the wild beasts that inhabit the desert, the angels that support him, his arch-rival, Satan and, supremely, God the Father himself who always accompanies those he calls into life's waste places.

The desert – a devastating place

Picture Jesus reaching the Judean desert – a thirty-five by fifteen-mile stretch of wilderness that is so terrifying that it's popularly known as 'The Devastation'. See him surrounded by long stretches of yellow sand, crumbling, blistering, peeling limestone, scattered shingle, hills that look like dust heaps and bare, jagged rocks. Imagine him pacing up and down on ground shimmering and glowing with heat as intense as a furnace; ground that sounds hollow to the footsteps; ground from which towers contorted strata – where seemingly warped and twisted ridges run in all directions. Picture him exploring terrain that leads to a spectacular cliff-edge – a 1200-foot drop of limestone and flint which, via a series of crags and precipices, eventually touches the Dead Sea.[4]

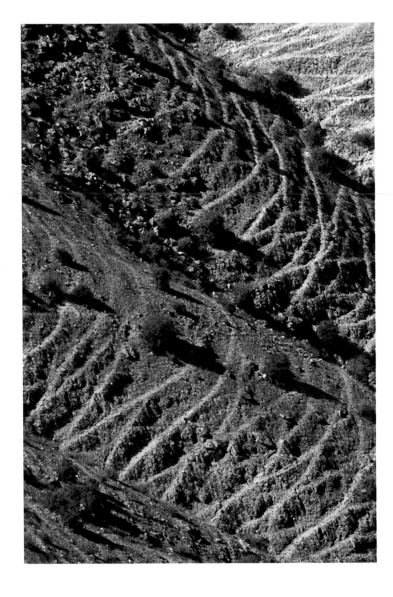

Imagine him sleeping, night after night, under the black, velvet, star-studded vault of heaven. Picture him waking, morning after morning, to the kaleidoscope of colour created by the sunrise. The silence seeps into him. It grips him. It draws him deeper and deeper into the reality of his Father's immortal Baptismal affirmation:

'You are the Beloved.
You are my Beloved.
I love you, not for anything you have done
nor for anything you will do in the future
but simply because you are.'

Truths like these trickle from Jesus' head into his heart. They stun him. They intoxicate him. They draw from him a heart-response that results in an indescribable, indestructible re-union with the Father. From this felt oneness a motto is conceived: 'I have come to do your will, O God' (Hebrews 10:7).

The motto provides him with the answer to the question that has been exercising him since he left the Jordan: '*How* am I going to win the world for the Father?' He's been turning this question over in his mind as he's walked and slept and heralded each new day. It's vital that he does so. The Spirit has thrust him into the desert to force him to think strategically. The way ahead is fraught with difficulties and dangers. Just as steel must go through fire to prove its strength, so God's Messiah must endure the fierce testing of the desert. The Spirit intends that Jesus will emerge from the test with clarity of vision and clear goals; equipped and empowered for the challenges ahead. The leader of the opposition party in God's Parliament[5] has other ideas,

---

Warped and twisted ridges run in all directions.

however. So, before his motto has time to dry on the parchment of his heart, Satan sidles alongside the Saviour and attempts to erase it.

The desert – a place of temptation

We know how the Enemy works. Scripture tells us. He is 'as subtle as the serpent, violent as the dragon, ruthless as the lion, deceptive as the angel of light . . . [He] is the murderer of [people's] spirit . . .'[6] Satan attacks people's minds with doubts and fears. He assails people's spirits with lust and pride. He assaults people's bodies with disease and torture.[7] We have experienced such wiles for ourselves. We know that he pesters and oppresses, beguiles and torments. He dresses up lies so that they masquerade as truth. He distorts the truth in such a way that our minds become befuddled and bemused. He's cunning, he intimidates, he fills us with fear and forces on us a fixation with self.

'Look after Number One,' he whispers to Jesus. 'Use your miraculous powers to make life more comfortable for yourself. Turn these stones into bread . . .'

Jesus hasn't eaten for six weeks. Satan's suggestions sound so sensible, so plausible, so right – on one level. Yet, on another level, they're questionable. Jesus is saturated with divine love. His fresh encounter with his Father motivates and inspires him. The battle of the mind begins. 'My motto is: "I've come to do your will, O God." So how can it be right to use my miraculous powers for me? They're to be used as the Father directs, not as I decide. But I'm hungry, faint, full of fear. . . .' Is this the kind of war that rages in his mind and heart before his will comes to the rescue with a resounding: 'Away from me, Satan' (Matthew 4:10)? Probably. The Jesus of the wilderness is the human Jesus – tempted in every way we're tempted; suffering sorely as he's tempted (Hebrews 2:18).

'Impress that clamouring crowd. Jump from the pinnacle of the temple. They'll love it. They'll flock to you. It's the kind of thing they expect . . .', the Tempter whispers again. Does he also fill Jesus with fear of failure? Does he force Jesus to focus on the seeming impossibility of the task? A lion tears at its prey. Does Satan tear at Jesus' heart and will creating inner havoc, smothering him with a blanket of despair, tying his mind in knots so that he can no longer think clearly? Probably. Such phenomena bear the hallmarks of the Enemy's tactics.

'Come over to my side. I'm the Prince of the world. I'll stop competing with you and give you what you want: the world and its people.'

What an alluring suggestion for a man now weakened by fasting and wearied with so many suggestions and counter suggestions. But he's the Beloved. He's focused on Love. He's been strengthened and renewed by it. The Father's love has elicited a response of reciprocal love: 'I've come to do *your* will, O God.' Such love is strong as death. Love for the Father reigns. From somewhere deep within, a surge of strength rises. Dislodging the debris of doubt, fear and the desire to capitulate, it erupts as a definitive resolve:

I refuse to live for self
I refuse to seek popularity
I will not crave for possessions
I refuse to seek power
So 'beat it Satan'.[8]

Round one of a life-long battle is over. Jesus returns to the still-hungry crowd transformed, refined, triumphant, energised: not simply Spirit-filled but Spirit-empowered, purposeful, like a well-shot arrow speeding towards its target.

The desert – a place of solitude

But Jesus never forgot the value or the wonder of the wilderness. Throughout his earthly ministry, he seeks solitude – retreating to places where, in the silence, he is reassured of his belovedness, where he immerses himself in the Father's love, where that love takes the sting out of the wounds inflicted on him by friends and enemies alike (see Matthew 14:23; Mark 6:6). His ingenuity finds places where he can glean God's perspective before making crucial decisions (Mark 9:2; Luke 6:12). He withdraws to places where he can open himself afresh to God's strength and wisdom and direction as he prepares for particular tasks or as he recovers from them (Mark 1:35).

These times of solitude re-charged his emotional, spiritual and physical batteries. Befriending and working with people syphons off energy that needs to be replenished. And Jesus is almost always surrounded with people.

> Besides his disciples, [he] was rarely without a crowd around him. His own personal space was constantly invaded – not just in terms of time but in actual physical contact. Jostled and pushed by the throng (Mark 5:31), forced to preach from a borrowed boat in order to distance himself a little from the growing crowd on the shore (Matthew 13:2), the picture builds up of someone under incessant pressure.[9]

He ensures that priority is given to such away days. Throughout his life he fleshes out the resolve he's made in the wilderness. His life is governed by his motto: 'I have come to do your will, O God.' As Sister Margaret Magdalene reminds us: He is 'not in bondage to the need to achieve, nor neurotic about the success of his mission, nor puffed up by popularity, he is free.'[10]

Because he is free, he flatly refuses to submit to 'the tyranny of the urgent'.[11] He refuses to permit his disciples or the crowd or the Pharisees to dictate the agenda. He lets God set the agenda and he says a firm 'No' to anything that is clearly not from God.

The desert – a symbolic place

Jesus not only learned the value of the terror and the wonder of the actual desert and substitute deserts, places of solitude, his life was also formed by that other desert I mentioned in the Introduction – the inner desert or, the symbolic desert, as it is sometimes called.

The 'symbolic desert' refers to any place where the landscape of the spirit, our inner landscape, is reminiscent of the bleakness, the barrenness and the beauty of the actual desert – any place, for example, where we are stripped of the resources we normally rely on, those places where we are tested almost beyond our endurance. It might be an internal place where emotional emptiness yawns, where loneliness haunts us or where the soul feels as parched and dry as cracked soil that cries out for water. The 'symbolic desert' might be an experience of mental anguish or dis-ease that creates havoc of the heart. It might take the form of a paralysis of the soul, a weakening of the body or an oppression of the spirit. The symbolic desert is any situation of helplessness, hopelessness and terror. It is any place that forces us to make a clean break with the past. It is also a place of wonder, a place where we encounter God in the depths of our being, a place where fresh revelations change the direction of our lives, a place where God whispers words of tenderness in the ears of our heart: 'I am now going to allure her; I will lead her into the desert and speak tenderly to her' (Hosea 2:14).

In his earthly pilgrimage, Jesus became as familiar with the symbolic desert as with the actual desert. For him, the stripping associated with the symbolic desert began at the moment of conception. As Paul's hymn of praise reminds us:

> Christ Jesus . . . had equal status with God but didn't
> think so much of himself that he had to cling to the
> advantages of that status no matter what. Not at all.
> When the time came, he set aside the privileges of deity
> and took on the status of a slave, became human. It was
> an incredibly humbling process. He didn't claim special
> privileges. Instead, he lived a selfless, obedient life and
> then died a selfless, obedient death – and the worst kind
> of death at that: a crucifixion.
>
> (Philippians 2:6–8)[12]

In other words, Jesus stepped straight from the spaciousness and
perfection of Paradise into the desert-like darkness of a woman's
womb. Having peeled off the privileges of deity, he squeezed
himself into the limitations of our humanity. The Creator of
mankind became a human embryo. The severity of this stripping
spanned the womb and the tomb and re-shaped him physically
and emotionally more than anyone before or since has been
shaped.

The symbolic desert re-shaped Jesus emotionally because it is
not only a place of stripping, it can be a place of terror. Was
Mary's womb a terrifying home for Jesus? Possibly – at least for
part of the time. Some kind of consciousness exists from the
moment of conception. The first three months of the foetus' life
are crucial. Emotions that grip the mother affect the unborn
child also. Far from being cushioned from them, the foetus feels
their full impact.

When Mary learned that she was to become Jesus' mother,
she was filled with fear. Fear must have dogged her as she came
to terms with the secret of her strange pregnancy: fear of gossip,
fear of rejection, fear of stoning, fear that she might have been
dreaming: that the revelation was not real.

Inside this bundle of fear lay a gestating seed. Having so

recently removed God's glory, the uniform of heaven, the now-naked Son of God tosses and turns to the drum-beat of his mother's dread. From the earliest possible phase of his earthly life, then, the desert of the soul equipped him with an understanding of, and an empathy with, those people who are too great to number for whom, similarly, the womb gave rise to a primal scream of terror rather than a primal dream of shalom, well-being.

The desert – a place of abandonment

Did this primal experience of fear re-surface in Gethsemane, on the Via Dolorosa, at Golgotha, on the Cross? Possibly. And worse. On the Cross, Jesus experiences the real terror of the desert – the feeling of abandonment, the fear that God himself has deserted him. In the psalmist's cry that commentators believe Jesus echoed on the Cross:

'My God, my God, why have you forsaken me?
  Why are you so far from saving me,
  so far from the words of my groaning?
O my God, I cry out by day, but you do not answer,
  by night, and am not silent . . .'

There on Golgotha, the place of the skull, he experienced the greatest transformation the desert has effected on anyone:

I am a worm and not a man,
  scorned by men and despised by the people.
All who see me mock me;
  they hurl insults, shaking their heads: . . .

I am poured out like water,
  and all my bones are out of joint.

My heart has turned to wax;
  it has melted away within me.
My strength is dried up like a potsherd,
  and my tongue sticks to the roof of my mouth;
  you lay me in the dust of death.
Dogs have surrounded me;
  a band of evil men has encircled me,
  they have pierced my hands and my feet.
I can count all my bones;
  people stare and gloat over me.
They divide my garments among them
  and cast lots for my clothing.

                    (Psalm 22:1,2,6,7; 14–18)

There, the Creator became the Redeemer:

> Today he who hung the earth upon the waters is hung
>   upon the Cross.
> He who is King of the angels is arrayed in a crown of
>   thorns.
> He who wraps the heaven in clouds is wrapped in the
>   purple of mockery.
> He who in Jordan set Adam free receives blows upon
>   his face.
> The Bridegroom of the Church is transfixed with nails.
> The Son of the Virgin is pierced with a spear.[13]

> Today a tomb holds him who holds the creation in the
>   hollow of his hand;
> a stone covers him who covered the heavens with glory.
> Life sleeps and hell trembles,
> and Adam is set free from his bonds.[14]

The desert – a place for us

Since God's very own Son was transformed so radically by the desert, since it was in the actual or the symbolic wilderness that his life-motto crystallised, his life-goals clarified, he was envisioned and empowered; since, in solitude, he received God's perspective on his ministry and was re-energised by love, perhaps we should not be surprised when our own pilgrimage takes us into desert-like places? Instead of feeling guilty or afraid to admit that we are wandering around in the trackless wastes of the spiritual wilderness, perhaps, like Jesus, we should accept, with humility and versatility, the worst and the best the wilderness offers? Perhaps such an attitude would enable us to look back on our desert experiences with awe and gratitude? Perhaps it would better enable us to learn the desert's lessons with eagerness?

Certain soul-searching questions help us to unearth the desert's positive contribution to our pilgrimage:

- Why am I in this place? Could it be that I am here because, like Jesus, I need to seek solitude?
- Could it be that God has invited me here to give me a fresh experience of his love?
- Who or what is setting the agenda of my life? Me? My colleagues? The organisation for which I work? Personal ambition? A competitive spirit? Greed? Pride? Or God?
- What is the motto that governs my attitudes and behaviour?
- Do I need to ask God for the gift of discernment so that I know when thoughts and desires and suggestions come from the Enemy? Do I need to be shown when I am suffering from oppression rather than from depression so that I can combat the Enemy of souls in the authoritative way Jesus dealt with him?

Such questions sharpen our thinking and increase the self-awareness needed if we are to grow rather than faint in the desert.

God sometimes needs to push us into the desert, for example, until we have learned the lesson both William Barclay and Sister Margaret Magdalene teach so faithfully:

> It may well be that we often go wrong simply because we never try to be alone. There are certain things which a [person] has to work out alone. There are times when no one else's advice is any good . . . There are times when a [person] has to stop acting and start thinking. It may be that we make many a mistake because we do not give ourselves a chance to be alone with God.[15]

> A life without a lonely place, that is, a life without a quiet centre, easily becomes destructive and, we might add, shallow, dissipated and lacking in any sense of direction. We get nowhere if we fear to walk alone. The busier life is, the more need there is for a still centre; a place deep within us to which we can withdraw after the day-to-day buffeting and storms; a place where we can reflect on experience and try to make sense of life; a place where we can mull over events and savour them more fully; a place where, above all, we can listen . . . to what others are saying verbally or non-verbally, to what our feelings and fears are saying to us, and to what God is saying through circumstances, through people, through creation and his word spoken in the depths of our being. All these things pass us by, like views from the window of an express train, if we do not learn to stand still at disciplined intervals and do some stock-taking and viewing.[16]

We may be busy, busy, busy in God's service and yet have no deep-down awareness that God loves us uniquely. Yet the Father refused to allow Jesus to ride on such a spiritual roller-coaster.

The Spirit drove Jesus into the wilderness after the Father had reminded him that he was a much-cherished child.

In today's spiritual climate, we may find ourselves drawn into the desert so that God can whisper tender words into our love-hungry hearts in an environment where we are freed to receive it – a place where we have rid ourselves of the clutter of other loves. The divine desert-dweller knows how vital this is for our survival. Only when we are rooted and grounded in love will we discover the resilience and the desire to resist the Tempter and place our faltering footsteps into the footprints of Christ.

Or we may find ourselves wooed into the desert because certain temptations threaten to knock us off course by distracting us, occluding our vision of God or encouraging us to become self-absorbed. They will almost certainly be variations on the theme of Jesus' temptations: to seek popularity and possessions, prestige and power, to let life revolve around self rather than around God and others. The above questions may help us sift and process these temptations and give us the courage Jesus had to send Satan packing. They are questions to toy with as we prepare to journey alongside heroes and heroines of the Faith who blazed a trail through the desert. Like us, they were less than perfect. Like Jesus, they were transformed by the desert experience. Like them, we, too can be transformed by all those experiences that seem as grim and rugged, as spectacular and overwhelming as the physical wilderness. In her moving allegory, *Hind's Feet on High Places*, Hannah Hurnard assures of this.

The heroine in the story is Much-Afraid, a member of the Fearing Family. She lives in the Valley of Humiliation. For several years Much-Afraid serves the Chief Shepherd whose flocks are pastured in the Valley of Humiliation. Content though she is, in very many ways, she grows increasingly conscious that certain handicaps spoil the picture of the Chief

Shepherd that others gain through her. She is a cripple for one thing. She also has a twisted mouth that disfigures her face and impedes her speech. The Chief Shepherd comes for her, takes her on a long, healing journey to the 'high places' that symbolise the inner journey we have focused on in this chapter. At first, Much-Afraid is excited, overwhelmed – then dismayed as the Chief Shepherd warns her:

> 'Much-Afraid . . . all My servants on their way to the High Places have had to make [a] detour through this desert. . . . Here they have learnt many things which otherwise they would have known nothing about. Abraham was the first of My servants to come this way. . .'[17]

Our next task, then, is to observe how the Chief Shepherd used the desert to transform that great man of faith and father of us all, Abraham himself.

We may find ourselves *drawn into the desert.*

Two

Abraham

Friend of God,
Father of Multitudes

All kinds of tales have been woven around Abram's early years. Like this one: When Abram was born, his father was the commander of the armies of Nimrod. Because a vivid star that obliterated all other stars announced Abram's birth, Nimrod felt threatened. 'The baby must be murdered,' he resolved. Someone hid Abram in a cave – and saved his life. Standing at the cave's mouth one day, Abram, now a youth, gazed at the desert. The sun was just rising. 'Surely the sun is God, the Creator!' he gasped as he fell to his knees and worshipped the glorious, golden ball. Imagine his disgust at sundown when the horizon swallowed the golden ball. 'The author of creation can't set!' he protested. Within hours, he was watching the moon smile from a navy-blue sky. 'The moon must be God and the stars his host!' he surmised. Kneeling down, he adored the silent, silver ball-with-a-face. Night faded, day dawned, the moon disappeared, the sun reappeared. Worship turned sour again: 'These heavenly bodies are no gods, for they obey law. I'll worship him who imposed the law upon them,'[1] Abram resolved. From that day, so the story goes, a conscious search for the Creator became the driving force of his life.

Perhaps legend contains more than a kernel of truth? Abram was clearly one of God's chosen ones (Genesis 18:18) – the forefather to whom God's affirmation of Jeremiah applied: 'Before I formed you in the womb I knew you, before you were born I set you apart; I appointed you as a prophet to the nations' (Jeremiah 1:5).

When God chooses us, he plants in us the desire and ability to respond to his love. As Maria Boulding explains:

> All your love, your stretching out, your hope, your thirst, God is creating in you so that he may fill you. It is not your desire that makes it happen, but his. He longs through your heart . . . In your prayer God is seeking you and himself creating the prayer; he is on the inside of the longing . . . God's longing for us is the spring of ours for him.[2]

Did Abram's fascination for the Creator come under threat from rival gods as he grew up in Ur of the Chaldees? Almost certainly. The city was the principal centre of the worship of the moon god, Nanna, and the Babylonian god, Sin, for one thing. With a father whose reputation for being an idol worshipper was widespread and notorious,[3] Abram could scarcely escape the lure of polytheism, for another. Ur was also a prosperous place to live. The false gods of materialism and consumerism, prestige and power, popularity and possessions were ever present persuading an impressionable youth that these gods held in their hands the secret of happiness and success.

Yet the flicker of Abram's yearning for God was not snuffed out. Although this city throbbed with the thrills of commerce, hummed with political intrigue and pulsated with colour and

Who is the choreographer that paints the sky?

culture and the craftsmanship of potters and sculptors, wood-carvers and artists, Abram's longing for God seems to have been fanned into a flame. When God's finger beckoned and God's whisper begged him to leave his life of luxury, unquestioningly, trustingly, Abram abandoned his life to the Creator. Together with Terah, his father, and Sarai, his wife, Abram began an outer journey and continued an inner journey that was to last the rest of his life. He had no map in his hand as he set out into the great unknown. He didn't even know where he was going. All he knew was that he was called by God and that, for some strange reason, he was being given the grace to go.

The desert – the place of revelation

What does Abram know about God as he sets out on this life-long journey? Little or nothing, it would seem. He knows that, as water draws a thirsty deer, so God draws him. He certainly doesn't know that this God frequently calls his loved ones into the desert so that, stripped of all other props and loves, they can be uniquely open to all his overtures of love and attentive to his whisper.

God unveils his nature through the sights and sounds and shapes and textures he has made. Did the wonders of the wilderness put questions in Abram's mind:

- What kind of Being must he be who creates cloudless, blue skies in the day and a star-studded sky at night?
- Who is the choreographer that paints the sky pink at sunrise and rose-gold at sunset?
- What landscape gardener creates furrows that form in a rich, shifting sea of sand as well as the shapes of sand dunes?
- What architect planned such an array of rocky gorges and forested mountain slopes, undulating, fissured hills and unforgettable rock formations?

- What artist produces such a kaleidoscope of changing colours and harmonising hues when the sun plays on the upturned faces of humpy hillocks and lofty mountain peaks?
- What craftsman created contour and texture, the folds of the mountains, the sleek coats of sheep and goats, the elegance of the ibex, the comical lurching of the camel?
- What composer orchestrates the soughing of the wind, the bleating of the sheep, the braying of the donkey, the laughter of a child?
- What kind of conductor insists on silence – that deep-down stillness that penetrates everything and everyone in the desert?
- What kind of wizard conjures up the magic of springtime when tangles of wild flowers cover the barren earth with a riot of colour?

Did the desert teach him that God is mighty and magnificent, full of splendour, strength and sensitivity, full of fun and compassion; as concerned about intimate and intricate detail as about the final effect of the object he is crafting? Did he discover that the desert is a place where the soul is saturated with a sense of the felt presence of God:

At sunset a great serenity sets in, as though nature were obeying a sudden sign from God.

The wind which has howled all day ceases, the heat dies down, the atmosphere becomes clear and limpid, and great peace spreads everywhere, as though man and the elements wanted to refresh themselves after the great battle with the day and its sun.

With your work finished and the caravan halted, you stretch out on the sand with a blanket under your head and breathe in the gentle breeze which has replaced the dry, fiery day-time wind.

Then you leave the camp and go down to the dunes for prayer. Time passes undisturbed. No obligations harass you, no noise disturbs you, no worry awaits you: time is all yours. So you satiate yourself with prayer and silence, while the stars light up the sky.[4]

Did Abram take time out to pray in this way? If so, was his knowledge of God increasing his desire for God? Probably. And such longing is often challenged. The challenge comes quite frequently from one's nearest and dearest.

The desert – a place of difficulty

Is this what happens to Abram? The desert is not only a place full of wonder, not only a place where, immersed in the grand silence, God's presence can be keenly felt and his voice clearly heard, the desert is also riddled with difficulties. Does Abram's family complain when the going becomes tough? They have, after all, exchanged the security of their safe, walled city for the perils of life in wastelands. They have also exchanged plenty for poverty. Nestled, as it was, between two magnificent and near-parallel rivers, the Tigris and the Euphrates, and in terrain ingeniously criss-crossed with canals, Ur's half million inhabitants were rightly proud of their crops. In the desert, however, Abram and his entourage were forced to forage for food for themselves.

Do the family suffer from a mounting sense of loss as time goes on? Does this threaten to knock them off balance as the full effect of being stripped of all the props they formerly took for granted sinks in? Do they grieve for friends, familiarity, and status? Are they sometimes overwhelmed by the relentlessness of the journey? Do they feel frustrated by the frequent pitching and striking of camp, the regular making and repairing of tents, the need to hunt for, cook and clear up foodstuffs, the need to travel, oh, so slowly? How do they cope with the extremes of temp- erature: the soaring, searing heat of the day and the contrasting chill of the night, the bewilderment of not knowing whether they are nearing journey's end or merely moving into its beginning? Do they pine for the culture they previously enjoyed and the cut and thrust of city life? Do they question whether Abram's call was truly from God or a figment of his fertile imagination? Does Terah mourn the loss of fellowship with other idol worshippers? Are they dogged by tiredness?

In all probability, some or all of these factors cause them to call a premature halt to the pilgrimage. In Haran, we watch them dismantling their tents and settling in this secure, flourishing centre of commerce and idol worship that seems so reminiscent of the homeland they have left. In Haran, do we witness Abram's heart being torn in two by a conflict of loyalties: the Middle Easterner's fierce sense of filial responsibility to his earthly father (it seems probable that he lingered in Haran for his father's sake[5]) and the longing in his heart to follow the beckoning finger of God? Do we watch him journeying into an inner desert that was every bit as bleak as the actual desert? Or does this first phase of the desert experience highlight a tug-of-war of a different kind? Is Abram being drawn by God on the one hand and tugged in the opposite direction by his addictions? An addiction is something that possesses us in such a way that we become enslaved to it, we lose our inner freedom and sense of well-being without it. Addictions can also be behaviour patterns that hook us, give rise to compulsive behaviour and create inner havoc when we are denied access to them. Is Abram addicted to wealth, the accumulation of possessions – to materialism? In Haran, he amasses a large number of this world's goods. Even so, God goes on loving him. Love gives of itself in its entirety to the loved one. So God, who allured Abram into the desert to convince him of this love, repeats his call and adds a string of promises:

> 'Leave your country, your people and your father's household
> and go to the land I will show you.
>> I will make you into a great nation
>> and I will bless you;
>> I will make your name great,
>> and you will be a blessing.
>> I will bless those who bless you,
>> and whoever curses you I will curse;
>> and all peoples on earth
>> will be blessed through you.'
>
> (Genesis 12:1,2)

And Abram, whose knowledge of God is, as yet, so slight, believes that God will, indeed, fulfil these promises. With awe, the writer of the Epistle to the Hebrews comments on Abram's child-like faith: 'By faith Abraham, when called to go to a place he would later receive as his inheritance ... went, even though he did not know where he was going' (Hebrews 11:8).

Taking his sterile wife, Sarai, his nephew, Lot, the slaves and servants, flocks, herds and his wealth with him, he sets out for Canaan once more.

The desert – a place of encounter

What passes through Abram's mind now? Why does he head for Shechem? Does he turn over and over in his memory those mind-blowing promises God had made: 'I will make you into a great nation . . .'. 'I will bless you . . .', 'I will make your name great . . .'? Did his meditation, there in the vastness, the awesomeness and the stillness of the desert cause his heart to bow in wonder and love, praise and humility? Such a scenario seems probable. By the time he reaches Shechem, he is ready to move on a notch in his relationship with God. Shechem (Genesis 12:6) was sandwiched between the Sea of Galilee and the Dead Sea. The sanctuary lay at the junction of five mountain-flanked valleys – one third of the way down the ridge of hills that curves from Haifa in the north to Beersheba in the south. Here, by the great oak tree of Moreh, Abram discovers that the desert is a place of encounter with God himself. Here God actually appears to Abram. Was this their first face to face encounter? Possibly. The experience was so overwhelming, so other-worldly that worship wells up within Abram's heart. Here on this holy ground, God seems to whisper: 'It's not enough to be drawn by me, to respond to me, to discover what kind of Being I am, to be aware of my Otherness and my Holiness, I want to give you something more. I want you to know me, to enjoy intimacy with me.'

Watch while Abram expresses the inexpressible – gratitude, adoration, love and praise – in the only way he knows how: by using his hands and heart, his senses and imagination, to build an altar where his whole being can immerse itself in God. Ponder God's response. As Paul reminds us, he credited Abram's faith 'as righteousness' (Romans 4:9).

How does Abram feel as he tears himself away from this sacred place and nudges his way through a series of awesome, terrifying, deep-cut valleys framed by heavily forested hills? What engages his mind? Could it be the amazing promise God made at Shechem: 'To your offspring I will give this land'? Probably. In the remote, sparsely populated, stunningly still place, Bethel, the immensity and generosity of God's love as much as God's grandeur gives birth to yet another burst of praise and another altar (Genesis 12:8). At this altar, he pauses and calls on the name of the One who is fast becoming his most fascinating friend.

The song of praise seems to die a sad death on his lips, however, and his deepening friendship with God seems to be

Tamarisk trees near Beersheba.

imperilled when, on the next lap of his journey, he finds his faith sorely tested. Famine forces him to take his entourage into Egypt and to settle there. Faith turns to fear as he approaches the land of plenty. Fearing the Egyptians would fall for Sarai's staggering beauty and fearing the Egyptians would kill him to possess her, Abram forces Sarai to lie: 'Say you are my sister,' he insists, 'so that I will be treated well . . . and my life will be spared' (Genesis 12:13).

Does he exchange the actual desert for the desert of the soul at this point in his life? Does he seek refuge in his addiction once more? Probably. He emerges from Egypt encumbered by accumulated wealth. Why does he drag all these possessions back to Bethel? Is he deliberately retracing his footsteps? Is he expressing a desire to resume his pilgrimage? We don't know. We do know that God pours compassion on him, comes to him, stays alongside him and consoles him: 'Don't be afraid, Abram. . . . I'm your King . . . *your greatest treasure*' (Genesis 15:1, emphasis mine).

Here in the desert, he learns that even when he fails, the ever-faithful God will never fail him. Here, in the desert, he discovers that, becoming God's friend is, at best, a gradual process. The life of turning from self with all its addictions, to God in all his purity and love must be lived out 'in all its three tenses'[6]: 'I have become God's friend, I'm still in the process of being turned around by him and, one day, I will have turned to him irrevocably, holding nothing back.' God goes on to give Abram an opportunity to commit himself afresh to the friendship: 'for better, for worse, for richer, for poorer, in sickness and in health'.

The desert – the place where friendship is cemented and tested

'Let's commit ourselves to one another for ever. I'll make you fruitful. I'll give you a new name: Abraham, father of many. I'll give you and your descendants the whole of the Land of Canaan. I'll give Sarai a new name, too: Sarah – which means "princess". She will be the mother of nations. Meanwhile you'll express your willingness to consecrate yourself to me by being circumcised. All the male members of your family after you must similarly be circumcised.'

At the age of 99, Abram, doubtless revelling in his new God-given name, Abraham, the father of nations, says yet another resounding 'yes' to God: the newly-initiated rite of circumcision is performed on him as on every male member of his household. But the picture is not one of pure joy. Abraham harbours a heartache that, like his addiction, holds him in its grip and sets up an inner struggle. On the one hand 'even though he was past age – and Sarah herself was barren . . . he considered him faithful who had made the promise' (Hebrews 11:11,12), on the other hand, the practicalities bog him down: 'O Sovereign LORD, what can you give me since I remain childless . . . You have given me no children; so a servant in my household will be my heir' (Genesis 15:2,3).

Like a variation on a theme, several other snippets of conversation Abraham has with God expose his perplexity and profound disappointment:

> God . . . said to Abraham, 'As for Sarai your wife, you are no longer to call her Sarai; her name will be Sarah. I will bless her and will surely give you a son by her. I will bless her so that she will be the mother of nations.'

Abraham falls face down when he hears this. He laughs out loud and mutters to himself: ' "Will a son be born to a man a hundred years old? Will Sarah bear a child at the age of ninety?" . . . Then God said, "Your wife Sarah will bear you a son, and you will call him Isaac" ' (Genesis 17:15–18).

Is Abraham recalling this conversation as he enjoys his siesta in the comparative cool of the entrance to his tent on that day when the three visitors come from God? Possibly. Is that not the reason why God promises: 'I will surely return to you about this time next year, and Sarah your wife will have a son' (Genesis 18:10)? Is this the occasion when Abraham becomes deeply convinced of the faithfulness of God – as the writer to the Hebrews puts it, when 'he considered him faithful who had made the promise' (Hebrews 11:11) that he will be the 'father of nations', that his offspring will be as numberless as the stars in the sky and the grains of sand on the seashore?

We can't be certain when Abraham believed that God's promise would be fulfilled. We do know that, a whole year later, he discovers that the desert is the place where God fulfils his promises: 'The LORD was gracious to Sarah as he had said, and the LORD did for Sarah what he had promised. Sarah became pregnant and bore a son to Abraham in his old age, at the very time God had promised him' (Genesis 21:1).

Picture Abraham, the old man, holding the promised child, his very own God-given son. In contrast, imagine his anguish when, some thirteen years later, God takes him even deeper into the desert of the soul by making it clear that, although he has been drawn by God from his youth up and although he has committed himself to God in the act of circumcision, God longs for even more commitment, even more love; that that commitment, like metal, must be tested. Listen to this heart-rending request:

> 'Take your son, your only son, Isaac, whom you love . . .
> Go to the region of Moriah. Sacrifice him there as a burnt
> offering on one of the mountains I will tell you about.'
>
> (Genesis 22:2)

Does Abraham struggle or hesitate? If he does, it is not disclosed. Instead, early next morning he takes his thirteen-year-old son on a three-day trek to a craggy outcrop – the present-day Dome of the Rock in Jerusalem. Sense the pit in his stomach as he trudges alongside his son for three whole days. What do they talk about? How does he feel as he gathers kindling for the holocaust? What kind of questions plague him? How deeply does bereavement bite into the flesh of his heart? Do tears stream down his face as he binds his son with ropes and lays him on the altar? Abraham, is, after all, a Middle Easterner and people in the Middle East express the intensity of their grief openly and movingly.

Now listen to the urgency of that spine-chilling cry from heaven that stays Abraham's hand and prevents him from sacrificing the most precious person in his life. Try to imagine how he feels as he hears the heavenly accolade:

> 'I swear by myself . . . that because you have done this and have not withheld your son, your only son, I will surely bless you and make your descendants as numerous as the stars in the sky and as the sand on the seashore . . . and through your offspring all nations on earth will be blessed, because you have obeyed me.'
>
> (Genesis 22:15–18)

The desert – the place where the friendship sometimes dies

Abraham goes down in history with a series of startling epitaphs:

> Abraham trusted God, and the Lord declared him good [righteous] in God's sight, and he was even called 'the friend of God'.
>
> (James 2:23 LB)

> By faith Abraham, when called to go to a place he would later receive as his inheritance, obeyed and went, even though he did not know where he was going.
>
> By faith he made his home in the promised land like a stranger in a foreign country; he lived in tents . . . For he was looking forward to the city with foundations, whose architect and builder is God . . .
>
> By faith Abraham, when God tested him, offered Isaac as a sacrifice. He who had received the promises was about to sacrifice his one and only son, even though God had said to him, 'It is through Isaac that your offspring will be

reckoned.' Abraham reasoned that God could raise the dead, and figuratively speaking, he did receive Isaac back from death.

(Hebrews 11:8,9,17)

In other words, God used the desert to transform this potentially worldly seeker-after-truth into a man of unshakeable faith – a through and through believer.

God has no favourites. He longs that everyone should bear the title 'friend of God'. He loves each person he has created as deeply and uniquely as he loved Abraham – that is why he plants within each individual the ability to respond to his love. Just as Abraham was drawn ever deeper into the immensity and mystery of God's fathomless love, so are those who reciprocate his love. Abraham's pilgrimage conceals a map that every pilgrim can confidently carry in their hearts. The map shows the way travellers must take *en route* for true, everlasting Love.

Our journey begins when we respond to God's call: 'Come!' After that call is heeded and heard, feverish activity often characterises the ongoing journey. We long to learn about the Creator. The desire might be so great that it feels like an insatiable thirst that prompts us to search for Living Water. We read about this Water, God himself, we discuss him, attend meetings and services where we can learn more about him, pray to him and even begin to yield ourselves to him. We store in the computer of our brain file after file of information about him. We might feel exhilarated – full of a sense of achievement and fulfilment. Gradually, however, there comes a time of desert dryness when knowing *about God* fails to satisfy. Now the heart-hunger yearns to *know him* in the sense of encountering him and developing a relationship with him. Although we might not recognise it, this is a call from God to take the risks involved in going deeper into the immensity of his love.

Often, during these early forays into the desert, we gain more from Bible meditation than Bible study. One by one, we take the insights we have stored in our minds and we ponder them, feast on them and discover that their richness trickles from our head into our heart. At the same time, we discover that prayer is essentially a love relationship with the Divine Lover. We no longer seek him, we discover the elixir of being found by him. The Franciscan, Boniface Maes, describes this phase of the journey well: 'The grace of God sometimes overflows like a river and invades the emotional powers of the soul . . . there follows spiritual intoxication, which is a breaking out of overwhelming tenderness and delicious intimacies greater than the heart can desire or contain.'[7]

Such spiritual intoxication, however, can mislead us. We can be beguiled into believing that we have 'arrived' spiritually speaking. But such euphoria rarely lasts. It evaporates because the love that wells up within us at such times needs to be tested and refined. The God who wooed us, called us, found us, led us, encountered us, overwhelmed us, now baffles us by appearing to play hide-and-seek. One moment he is there – large and loving as ever – the next minute he disappears. Mysteriously and persistently, he lures us deeper and deeper into the desert of desire – his desire for us and ours for him. At the same time, we may well feel that we have lost our way. No signposts indicate the path ahead. No tracks can be detected. So there is no turning back. We can only press on along the pathway that our own footsteps create. As we journey on, the ache in our hearts causes us to cry out for him because our senses can no longer discern him. All the time our longing for him grows greater. All the time, even though neither Bible study nor Bible meditation nor the prayer of contemplation satisfy the soul in the way they once did, the Divine Lover is increasing inside us what the mystics call a *capax dei*, a greater capacity for God. All the time, in the seeming emptiness of the desert, God is stripping us of other loves, gouging us out so that our longing for him becomes insatiable. When the time is ripe, he returns: we see him, we hear him, we sense him, we touch him, and we are overwhelmed by the joy of the renewed oneness with himself that he permits.

The way to such oneness almost always runs through the wastelands of the wilderness. Contemporary author, Thomas Green, writing of desert spirituality, makes a telling observation. He claims that, whereas Christian praying people relish the years of gleaning insights about God and the transition from knowledge to experience – that phase of the pilgrimage when prayer is spontaneous and joyful – few persevere when they are wooed into the wilderness. The reason is that 'they do not want to pay the price of growth'.[8] Unlike Abraham, they cannot tolerate the severity of the stripping of life's luxuries or the withdrawal from their addictions. 'Normally they do not abandon prayer or God altogether. They remain 'good' people. But they settle for a level of comfortable mediocrity: loving, but not too much; giving, but only within the comfortable limits they have set themselves.'[9] Others, however, do abandon the pilgrimage. Having enjoyed basking in the warmth of the sunshine of God's felt love, they cannot cope with the unpredictability of this elusive lover. They want a God who dances to their drum-beat rather than the God of Abraham who insists on calling the tune – the God who calls for complete commitment to himself. Such people often fall into the temptation of letting work for God fill the gap left by their abandonment of an ongoing relationship with him.

The more I am involved in the privileged ministry of listening to others, the more I am convinced that Thomas Green's insights deserve careful scrutiny. That is why I am closing this chapter with a series of questions that I invite readers to respond to:

- Where am I on this cyclical journey of faith?
- Ask yourself the questions on pages 32–33 and then look back on your life and ask yourself: How has my image of God changed?
- Do I spend much of my prayer time gleaning insights about God?
- Am I just beginning to experience his love in a deeper way and richer measure?
- Have I ever made a life-commitment to him? If so, does this life-commitment need underlining?
- Have I discovered that God is a God who appears to play hide-and-seek: sometimes allowing us to sense his presence, sometimes appearing to be strangely absent?
- Have there been occasions when I feel as though I am strangely lost in a spiritual wilderness?
- At such times, have I been able to echo Abraham's cry of faith: 'God will provide'?
- Like Abraham, do I sometimes find myself in a place of split loyalties? If so, what can I learn from Abraham and Sarah?
- Would I call myself a friend of God? Why?
- Am I prepared to pay the price of spiritual growth?
- Do the words of this desert song still resonate in my heart?

He won't let you stumble,
Your Guardian God won't fall asleep . . .
Yahweh's your Guardian,
Right at your side to protect you –
Shielding you from sunstroke
Sheltering you from moonstroke . . .
Yahweh guards you from every evil,
He guards your very life.
He guards you when you leave and when you return,
He guards you now, he guards you always.
(Psalm 121 – A Pilgrim Song)[10]

THREE

Moses

'A giant of all times'[1]
'A very humble man'[2]

He was born under sentence of death, yet he lived a full span, and more. He grew up amid the luxury of a royal court, yet he threw in his lot with slaves. Coddled and pampered by an absolute monarch, he joined the monarch's most persecuted victims. Trained in the strict tenets of a ritual conservatism, he became a revolutionary. Halting of speech he uttered words of sublime wisdom. In a world and a time of corruption, with little value placed on human life, he put forth a timeless and unexcelled code of ethics for the human race. Taken at birth from his people and their faith, he established their distinctive religion and moulded them into a nation. This was Moses . . .[3] – the 'man of God' who was sculpted by the desert.

Abraham dies. God's people become 'as numerous as the stars in the sky' (Deuteronomy 28:62). And Moses takes up the baton of leadership – but only after God has used a long sojourn in the desert to shape and re-shape this outstanding leader-in-the-making.

Unlike Abraham, Moses was not called into the desert. Fear forced him there: fear of Pharaoh, fear of the Egyptians, fear of the Hebrews, fear for his life. The fugitive who has just murdered an Egyptian (Exodus 2:11,12) suddenly exchanges the pomp and ceremony of Pharaoh's court for the sprawling sand-dunes of the Sinai desert: 'the vast and dreadful desert, that thirsty and waterless land, with its venomous snakes and scorpions . . .' (Deuteronomy 8:15).

What thoughts filled his mind as he trudged the four hundred miles that separated Egypt from Midian? Was he most aware of the actual desert whose wonder and terror engulfed him? Or was he more acutely aware of the desert of his soul: the fear that added wings to his feet, the anger that, like a forest fire, still blazed in his heart, the shame that his good intentions had backfired, the guilt that his hands were stained with blood, the sorrow that he had been unable to bid his family farewell; that they would have no idea where he was. Did he, perhaps, watch frequent action replays of his past? Did he recall the stories his mother and his sister had told him about the circumstances surrounding his birth, how he had been born and brought up in an emotional and symbolic desert?

Imagine this gifted, sorrow-filled, frustrated man moving ever deeper into the vast, grim desert. Imagine him caning himself over and over again. Imagine, too, how, little by little, the healing properties of nature seeped into his soul: the glow of the rose-gold sky that heralded and terminated each day, the serenity of the star-spangled sky at night, the timelessness of the great primeval crags, the spaciousness of the seemingly endless stretches of sun-scorched sand. Did the vastness and the emptiness, the grandeur and the wonder become for him fingers that patiently and persistently pointed him to the God the Hebrews revered? In the silence and solitude, peace and mystery of this deserted place, as year after year he communed with creation, could he, at last, begin to fathom the faith of his family that had eluded him in Egypt? Now that he had become a fugitive prince, no longer surrounded by temple priests and a plethora of Egyptian deities, could he see and hear and sense and touch insights that had seemed so elusive in his polytheistic youth?

Possibly. The stillness that is so profound in the desert that the traveller scarcely dares to breathe at times is, of itself, a language. Its cry, 'God, God, God . . .' echoes around mountain ranges, down gorges and through valleys. Such silence, the Desert Fathers were to claim, is the safest way to God.

The desert – a place of stripping

Another safe way to God is in the company of a fellow traveller who is more conversant with the desert than we are. Such a man was Jethro whose name means 'friend of God', and who now befriends Moses. Jethro and his seven daughters teach Moses Bedouin folk-lore and lifestyle. Moses needs their insights. After marrying one of the daughters, Zipporah, the former prince roams the desert with his father-in-law's flocks. He watches them and searches for the occasional patches of scrubland that are to be found in this parched, sun-blistered land. On his travels, he discovers water is the top priority of the desert.

Does he, then, marvel at the desert's miracle – oases like 'Elim' – that luscious place that boasted twelve springs and seventy palm trees where the Israelites were later to camp near the water (Exodus 15:27)? Do his family tell him of other water holes and encourage him to search for the 'desert seas': that other miracle of the desert that is created when heavy rain rushes down the mountain-sides in a flash flood and becomes trapped in gorges or between rocks?

The privileged prince soon discovers that he must not only find water in the desert but food also. He learns which plants are edible – like the hyssop herb – or like the caper: that plant with the exotic purple and white flower that looks like a sea anemone, defies the searing heat of the noonday desert sun, draws nourishment from seeming dry dust and is both delicious and nutritious, particularly when pickled.

The desert – a place of encounter

For forty years Moses lives as the Bedouins live and eats what they eat. He eats quail: those little birds that inhabit the Sinai desert and are such a delicious delicacy. Does he marvel as he watches huge flocks of these small, migratory birds fly over the Sinai desert *en route* from Arabia to summer in Europe? Does he watch them come to roost, exhausted, in the desert scrub or on open ground making them an easy catch?

He eats manna – that whitish resin-like fruit of the tamarisk tree that tastes like 'pure sugar with a hint of coriander'. And he eats the vitamin-rich fruit of the almond tree: the soft green outer casing that is a refreshing fruit in itself, and later the ripe and nourishing almond.

In so many ways, Moses becomes a Bedouin. Yet his dialogue with God on Mount Horeb betrays the fact that the past still haunts him. Here, forty years later, dwarfed as he is by the 7,400-foot-high Mount Horeb (Mount Sinai), does he feel soiled and guilty? Is he, perhaps, watching an action replay of the events that forced him to put such a vast distance between himself and Egypt? Is he recalling how he, the then powerful prince, full of his own importance, went to his own people, watched them 'at hard labour' and witnessed an Egyptian seize a whip with which he beat a Hebrew? Is he remembering how, 'glancing this way and that and seeing no-one, he killed [that] Egyptian and hid him in the sand' (Exodus 2:11,12)? Possibly – because, as he gazes at the breath-taking view that opens out before him: the vast, rugged range of gaunt mountain peaks, as the silence holds him in its grip, the Hebrews' God calls: 'Moses, Moses!'

His name echoes round the mountain range. Enveloped in holy fire God continues:

'I have indeed seen the misery of my people in Egypt. I have heard them crying out because of their slave drivers, and I am concerned about their suffering. So I have come down to rescue them from the hand of the Egyptians and to bring them up out of that land into a good and spacious land, a land flowing with milk and honey . . . So now, go. I am sending you to Pharaoh to bring my people the Israelites out of Egypt.'

(Exodus 3:4,7–10)

Do memories from the symbolic deserts of the past pour, like a flash-flood, into Moses' mind: the wilderness of his mother's womb, his abandonment as a baby, his rescue from the Nile, his privileged but isolated upbringing when he became privy to the wiles and ways of Pharaoh and his confidantes, his surreptitious contact with his blood relatives that alerted him to their sufferings, as well as the sight of his enslaved people, the blood of the Egyptian overseer he, himself, had butchered to death, his flight, his transformation from a potential slave to a privileged prince to a desert shepherd? Does he now piece the memories together as a craftsman pieces together fragments of stone to create a memorable mosaic? Does the realisation begin to dawn that the symbolic deserts have paved the way for this sudden call to become the shepherd of his people and God's people in the actual desert? Possibly. Even so, he struggles. Moses struggles and God persists. Before the burning bush, the compulsion and arrogance of earlier years melt and Moses balks at the challenge God gives him. 'Please send someone else!' (Exodus 4:13), he pleads, as so many desert sojourners have pleaded since.

The God of the desert appears not to hear. He persists. In his

View of Mount Sinai enjoyed by Moses.

hand the desert becomes the chisel with which he whittles away pride, arrogance and pretence (Deuteronomy 8:2). The result is startling. Later we read what Moses became: 'Moses was a very humble man, more humble than anyone else on the face of the earth' (Numbers 12:3).

Because the desert is the place of struggle, of revelation and of new beginnings, it is also a place of grace – undeserved, unasked-for strengthening, empowering love. Moses discovered that God never makes requests of a person without pouring into that person the grace he or she needs to utter a faltering 'yes'. In the desert, like countless others who were to come after him, Moses found that the wilderness is the place where we are gently and gradually converted by God in the sense that we are turned round; slowly but surely we place our own desires and compulsions behind us and in their place focus our attention on the God around whom we long that our world should increasingly revolve.

The desert – a place of miracles

The transformation doesn't happen in a hurry. While we are being re-shaped, God stays alongside us, consoling us, instructing us, forgiving us, opening our eyes further to the wonder of who he is: the God with whom nothing is impossible, the God of surprises, the God of miracles. So Moses' staff becomes a snake and then a staff again, his hand turns leprous but then is miraculously healed. God promises that he will endow Moses with power to do similar miracles. With the miracles come the portion of grace Moses needs to capitulate: to say his 'yes' to God. With God's grace, he gradually grows in stature.

Contrast the reluctant, cringing prophet-to-be of the desert with the giant-in-the-making who stands on the banks of the Sea of Reeds with the 600,000 Israelite men and the countless women and children who eventually escaped from Egypt (Exodus 12:37; Numbers 11:21). Picture the chaos. The Israelites suddenly find themselves sandwiched between the swirling waters of the Sea of Reeds on one side and all the chariots of Egypt 'with officers over all of them' in hot pursuit of them on the other side. Moses brings order into the chaos with his authoritative: 'Do not be afraid. Stand firm and you will see the deliverance the LORD will bring you today . . . The LORD will fight for you; you need only to be still' (Exodus 14:13,14).

Watch Moses co-partner God in the task of miracle-making. Stretching out his hand, the swirling waters divide to form two solid sea walls. A clearing emerges along which the Israelites escape. The Egyptians follow in hot pursuit. When they drive their chariots through the waters, though, Moses stretches out his hand again. The waters flood the clearing completely covering and drowning each and every chariot and horseman. 'Not one of them survived' (Exodus 14:28).

Phase one of the Israelites' enforced, prolonged desert retreat has begun. There, in the absence of luxuries or even seeming necessities, in the absence of creature comforts or securities of any kind, Moses gradually gleans an accurate image of God. Whereas, before the burning bush, we read of him hiding his face because he was afraid to look at God (Exodus 3:6), at the Sea of Reeds, he co-operates with the God of miracles. And on Mount Sinai we hear of God speaking with Moses 'face to face, as a man speaks with his friend' (Exodus 33:11). On Mount Sinai, too, he learns to pray the prayer of obedience.

The desert – a place of prayer

In response to God's call, Moses goes back to Egypt and, statesman that he is, negotiates with Pharaoh until, eventually, God's chosen people are set free from slavery. Now a new set of difficulties litter the wilderness.

The Children of Israel were not a hand-picked group of educated idealists with a burning passion for freedom. They were not therefore highly motivated to withstand hardship after hardship on their journey to the Promised Land.

> They were a simple people, born bondsmen, brought up without hope, who were suddenly jerked out of their grim but familiar life-pattern and thrust into a strange and dangerous nomadic existence. . . . Although Moses must surely have told them that the road would be long and hard, they had been thinking only in the limited terms of their day-to-day experience. Freedom [for them] meant immediate relief from rigorous labour and painful beatings.[4]

When miracles happened, like the Sea of Reeds parting at precisely the right moment, they sang lusty praises to God, and the women danced. When, three days later, having trekked through the intense, oppressive heat of the oven-hot desert, Moses failed them by taking them to Marah where the waters were too bitter to drink, they railed at him.

Faced with this crisis of leadership, Moses learns that prayer is not simply contemplating God or serving Yahweh, prayer also involves listening to the One who has called him. At Marah we read that 'Moses cried out to the LORD' (Exodus 15:25). He not only cries out, he listens to God's prompting: 'and the LORD showed him a piece of wood . . .' (v 25). As soon as Moses throws the wood into the waters of Marah, the bitterness disappears and the Israelites enjoy refreshing, sweet water.

Over and over again we read of Moses praying the prayer of enquiry: 'What am I to do with these people?' (e.g. Exodus 17:4). Over and over again we hear God making a specific response to a particular request: 'The LORD answered Moses' (Exodus 17:5).

But true prayer is more than contemplating, serving and listening to God. God created us to be in relationship with himself and, until our prayer includes intimacy with him, our hearts will never be satisfied.

Despite the demands of his calling, we see the desire for intimacy with the Holy One welling up in Moses from time to time – like on Mount Sinai. There, away from his clamouring, complaining people, in that place that filled him with awe, that place where God had already revealed the desires of his heart (Exodus 20), Moses is once again immersed in the grand silence of God: that silence that engulfs, draws and prompts us to stand still, to look up, to gaze, to behold the beauty and the majesty of God. Once again he is free to absorb the peace that pours from the pre-sunrise glow at the beginning of the day as much as from the still brightness of the moon at night. There, alone with the Holy One, the Eternal, the Infinite, the Transcendent One who had appeared to him, he attempts to express his inexpressible longing: 'If you are pleased with me, teach me your ways *so I may know you*' (Exodus 33:13 emphasis mine) Moses falteringly pleads one day. 'Now show me your glory,' he persists (v 18).

The Creator yearns to be known, that is, to enjoy intimacy with his creatures (Psalm 46:10). Delighting in his servant's request, he responds with those immortal, tender words: 'There is a place near me where you may stand on a rock . . .'

Protectively he adds: 'When my glory passes by, I will put you in a cleft in the rock and cover you with my hand until I have passed by. Then I will remove my hand and you will see my back; but my face must not be seen' (Exodus 33:21–23).

Evidence that the relationship between God and Moses has become more intimate is seen when, eventually, Moses descends from the jagged, rugged, God-graced mountain-top to the plain. Aaron and the Children of Israel saw it: 'his face was radiant because he had spoken with the Lord' (Exodus 34:29).

Doubtless Moses could have testified to the oneness with God Carlo Carretto describes – only more so:

> I feel him there, searching me out, coming to meet me, I feel him embracing me already, like someone who has been waiting for a long time, knowing that I would be coming.
>
> Filled with grateful love, I reach out to touch that beauty which is his beauty, I ponder the harmony which is his harmony, I stand spellbound by the newness which is his newness. And it is easy for me to say to him:
>
> > 'Bless Yahweh, my soul.
> > Yahweh, my God, how great you are!
> > Clothed in majesty and glory,
> > wrapped in a robe of light!'
> > (Psalm 104:1–4)[5]

Passionate, effective, world-changing intercession flows from this intimacy between God and the believer. And Moses was one of God's greatest intercessors.

Intercession is the prayer of making requests to God on behalf of others. Intercession has been well defined as 'standing before God with people on your heart'.[6] Intercession is the prayer of compassion, that is, the prayer that pours forth from the gut-level hurt we feel about a certain situation. 'Intercession is a costly loving of the world offered out of the depths of our lives'[7] – the prayer of involvement.

Listen to the boldness with which Moses intercedes.

While he is on the mountain receiving from God the tablets of stone on which the Almighty had written the Ten Commandments, the Israelites created the golden calf which they proceeded to worship. ' "Go down, because your people . . . have become corrupt . . ." ', God instructed Moses. ' "They are a stiff-necked people. Now leave me alone so that my anger may burn against them and that I may destroy them . . ." '

But Moses prays:

'O Lord . . . why should your anger burn against your people, whom you brought out of Egypt with great power and a mighty hand? . . . Turn from your fierce anger; relent and do not bring disaster on your people. . . .' Then the LORD relented and did not bring on his people the disaster he had threatened.

(Exodus 32:7–14)

Compassion for his people continues to consume Moses right up to the moment of his death. Just before he climbs Mount Nebo for the last time, he affirms the faithfulness of God and holds into the arms of the Faithful One those for whom he is concerned – the twelve tribes of Israel.

'I will proclaim the name of the LORD . . .
He is the Rock, his works are perfect,
    and all his ways are just.
A faithful God who does no wrong,
    upright and just is he.'

(Deuteronomy 32:3,4)

'Let Reuben live and not die . . .' [he begs].
'Be [Judah's] help against his foes!
Bless all [Levi's] skills . . .
    and be pleased with the work of his hands.'

(Deuteronomy 33:6,7,11)

Having prayed this caring prayer, God's giant gazes on the Promised Land that, like Abraham before him, he would inherit only through his descendants: Moses dies a mysterious death. On this poignant note the story does not end. Instead, a new chapter begins: 'Joshua . . . was filled with the spirit of wisdom because Moses had laid his hands on him' (Deuteronomy 34:9).

Joshua takes the baton from a Moses who is scarcely recognisable when compared with the arrogant prince he once was or the fugitive who fled into the desert. Now he is acclaimed as Israel's greatest prophet, the giant 'whom the LORD knew face to face, who did all those miraculous signs and wonders the LORD sent him to do in Egypt'; the one who displayed insurmountable power 'in the sight of all Israel' (Deuteronomy 34:11,12) yet who also goes down in history as the man who was 'more humble than anyone else on the face of the earth' (Numbers 12:3).

The desert – a place for us to negotiate

If we, too, would become people of prayer, as we observed in the last chapter, we must expect our pathway to God to take us through the desert – not the physical desert but the symbolic desert. As we saw in chapter one, the symbolic or inner desert is any situation where the landscape of the soul is reminiscent of the sea of sand and cracked, parched earth that characterises the actual desert. It might be a situation of hopelessness and helplessness, any situation where we watch the resources we normally rely on dwindle and dry up – any situation where we sense we have lost our way. Our own wilderness might be the emptiness of loss that comes through bereavement or redundancy, depression or burnout, illness or loneliness, post-accident trauma or marriage breakdown; failure of any kind. Alternatively our desert might be the desert of discouragement or confusion about prayer, weariness or disappointment or an awareness of our innate sinfulness to mention but a few twentieth-century deserts.

'What do I do when my pathway to God leads me into the waste places of the wilderness – when I seem to have lost my way?' That's a question Christians often ask from the depths of their pain and confusion. Because the desert was the school of prayer from which Moses emerged with such flying colours, there is value in letting Moses be our teacher.

He teaches us that, even when prayer seems difficult, dry or dull, we need to come to God: to pray the prayer of complaint, perhaps – or the prayer of despair.[8]

He teaches us, too, to surrender to God all that we have and all that we are. Such surrender is living prayer. While praying like this we may feel and hear and sense and see nothing. Yet such prayer might be the most pure prayer we ever pray. We pray, not for anything we expect to receive but because God is and we want to make a selfless, sincere offering of our heart to him. That is why prayer of this nature rises like sweet-smelling incense to the One who loves us eternally.

Moses also teaches us to hope, in the sense of depending on, God's promises and power. He challenges us to watch to see the way in which God's creative love will express itself at every twist and turn of the road. He teaches us, too, to look around every corner expecting the new mercies God constantly showers on us. Sometimes, for example, dryness in prayer points to the fact that we need to change the way we pray. In his mercy, God guides us into different, more effective ways of deepening our relationship with him.

God's giant also models the value of waiting. Few of us find it easy to believe that 'when you're waiting, you're not doing nothing. You're doing the most important something there is. You're allowing your soul to grow up' – you're becoming 'what God created you to be'.[9]

Yet Moses' life must sometimes have seemed like one long wait. He waited for the moment to ripen when he could deliver his people, he waited in the wilderness while he lived with the Bedouins, he waited and waited for Pharaoh to be ready to release the Hebrew slaves. The forty-year sojourn in the wilderness must have stretched his patience to the limit. He waited on Mount Sinai for the Ten Commandments, he waited for the Promised Land which he glimpsed but never entered. Yet his epitaph reads: 'No-one has ever shown the mighty power or performed the awesome deeds that Moses did in the sight of all Israel' (Deuteronomy 34:12).

Like Moses, the challenge that comes to us is to refuse to run away from the desert or to evade it by filling our life with activity, distractions or noise but rather to be present to it, to plumb the depths of its pain and emptiness and loneliness and, of course, to enjoy its wonder – not least the oases we sometimes stumble upon. As the little prince in Antoine de Saint-Exupery's story points out: 'The desert is beautiful . . . What makes the desert beautiful . . . is that somewhere it hides a well.'[10]

Each person's experience of the well will be different:

It seemed to me I was wandering in a desert with no end, with empty horizons and unattainable mirages which melted into nothing . . . a place where I could not find any water.

And then something came out of the silence . . . some-thing stirred with the chants . . . nothing tangible, nothing I could see – no, nothing like that . . . just something which moved out of the darkness, to enter into my soul and touch it with a kind of healing.

It was a presence in my desert . . . like dew silently filling the air and melting the cracked earth . . . I heard no voice – but that was of no importance . . . I was not suddenly overjoyed – no – but that was not important either. It only mattered that God has been in my desert, unbeknown to me . . . this is all that matters because with

God are the hidden wells of water.[11]

When we plod through the desert, although we may not realise it at the time, we are being changed; our prayer is being transformed. We are allowing God to be God. We no longer remain under the illusion that all we have to do is to pray 'Come!' and God comes. Now we know that in prayer, as in everything else, God is the one who takes the initiative. When the time is ripe, he will come – with his presence or his presents.

The hidden well water might come in the form of a companion – someone who will be to us what Jethro was to Moses, a spiritual Bedouin who has learned the art of thriving even in the inner desert; someone who can point out hidden dangers as well as expose the water-holes, the quails and the manna.

The hidden well water might be revealed as we learn that other lesson Moses teaches us – that of letting go. When something or someone is precious to us, the temptation is to cling. When we cling, our fists are clenched and we are unable to stretch out open hands to receive the new thing or person or insight God yearns to give. Moses learned, albeit with a struggle, to pray the prayer of relinquishment regularly – and so can we. As God himself challenges us:

'Stop dwelling on past events
and brooding over days gone by.
I am about to do something new;
this moment it will unfold.
Can you not perceive it?
Even through the wilderness I shall make a way,
and paths in the barren desert. . . .
for I shall provide water in the wilderness
and rivers in the barren desert. . . .'

(Isaiah 43:18–21)[12]

In other words Moses' example poses a series of questions: Am I prepared to abandon myself to the hands of the Lord of the desert as soft, malleable clay abandons itself to the hands of the potter? Am I willing to allow the Heavenly Potter to use the wheel of the desert to re-shape me? Am I prepared to allow the desert to purify even my prayer? Am I prepared, in my prayer, to let God do more and more while I do less and less? Dare I trust that, concealed in the seeming barrenness of my soul lie seeds that are germinating – seeds that will become the mature fruit of the Spirit? Am I prepared to believe that even my desert will blossom like the rose? Can I write desert songs of my own?

The desert – a Place of Worship

A Song of Moses
I will proclaim the name of the LORD.
  Oh, praise the greatness of our God!
He is the Rock, his works are perfect,
  and all his ways are just.
A faithful God who does no wrong,
  upright and just is he.

In a desert land he found him,
  in a barren and howling waste.
He shielded him and cared for him;
  he guarded him as the apple of his eye,
like an eagle that stirs up its nest
  and hovers over its young,
that spreads its wings to catch them
  and carries them on its pinions.
The LORD alone led him;
  no foreign god was with him.

                                   (Deuteronomy 32:3,4;10–12)

I will sing to the LORD,
  for he is highly exalted.
The horse and its rider
  he has hurled into the sea.
The LORD is my strength and my song;
  he has become my salvation.
He is my God and I will praise him,
  my father's God, and I will exalt him.
The LORD is a warrior;
  the LORD is his name.
Pharaoh's chariots and his army
  he has hurled into the sea.

(Exodus 15:1–4; 13)

Come, let's shout praises to Yahweh,
  raise the roof for the Rock who saved us!
Let's march into his presence singing praises,
  lifting the rafters with our hymns!

And why? Because Yahweh is the best,
  High King over all the gods.
In one hand he holds deep caves and caverns,
  in the other hand grasps the high mountains.
He made Ocean – he owns it!
  His hands sculpted Earth!

So come, let us worship: bow before him,
  on your knees before Yahweh who made us!
Oh yes, he's our God,
  and we're the people he pastures, the flock he feeds.

(Psalm 95: The Message)

FOUR

Elijah

Like Moses – Like Us

A 'second Moses' strides across the pages of history in the second half of the ninth century BC. As he steps out of obscurity into limelight's glare, he wears the prophet's habit: a camel-hair cloak. Like a well-stoked furnace, his heart blazes with zeal to bring God's people back to the way of Moses. Such zeal was sorely needed. Since Moses' demise, ten kings had progressively plunged Israel into spiritual darkness and near ruin. Moses' obituary claimed:

> Never has there been such a prophet in Israel as Moses. The LORD spoke with him face to face.
>
> No other prophet has ever done miracles and wonders like those that the LORD sent Moses to perform. . . .
>
> No other prophet has been able to do the great and terrifying things that Moses did in the sight of all Israel.[1]

But the kings' epitaphs make terrifying reading: 'He did evil in the eyes of the LORD, walking in the ways of his father and in his sin' (1 Kings 15:26). That's the summary of Nadab's reign, while of his assassin and successor, Baasha, it was written: 'He did evil in the eyes of the LORD, walking in the ways of Jeroboam and in his sin . . .' (1 Kings 15:34).

The nature of this sin is exposed in the condemnation of the next king, Elah. He provoked God's anger because he caused Israel to bow down to 'worthless idols' (1 Kings 16:13).

Elah's murderer, Zimri, reigned for only seven days, but one week was long enough to earn him the following obituary: 'He died, because of the sins he had committed, doing evil in the eyes of the LORD' (1 Kings 16:19).

His successor, Omri, fared no better: 'Omri did evil in the eyes of the LORD and sinned more than all those before him. He walked in all the ways of Jeroboam . . . and in his sin, which he had caused Israel to commit, so that they provoked the LORD, the God of Israel, to anger by their worthless idols' (1 Kings 16:25,26).

And, worst of all, Omri's successor, Ahab, is found guilty of doing even more evil and of provoking more anger from God than any of his predecessors:

> He not only considered it trivial to commit the sins of Jeroboam:
> he married Jezebel [Jeze-Baal], the daughter of Ethbaal king of the Sidonians
> he began to serve Baal and worship him
> he built a temple to Baal in Samaria
> he made an altar to Baal and put it in Baal's temple
> he also put up an image of the goddess Asherah (the 'wife' of Baal)
>
> (1 Kings 16:31–33)

> There was never a man like Ahab, who sold himself to do evil in the eyes of the LORD, urged on by Jezebel his wife. He behaved in the vilest manner by going after idols . . .
> (1 Kings 21:25)

All this idol worship flew in the face of Moses' clear instructions:

> Do not worship other gods, any of the gods of the peoples around you. If you do worship other gods, the LORD's anger will come against you like fire and will destroy you completely, because the LORD your God, who is present with you, tolerates no rivals.
>
> (Deuteronomy 6:14,15 GNB)

Despite this warning, on entering Canaan, the Israelites found that Baal-worship was the norm. Instead of shunning it and removing the idols, scores of them fell prey to this god's charms. As Lance Pierson explains:

> Baal-worship is easy for human nature to understand. You give the gods your sacrifice, and they look after you in return. It flatters human vanity: the larger your gift or the louder your chanting, the more impressed the gods will be. Worship is a materialist bargain: you pay your money and get your insurance cover; you do your bit, and then get on with the rest of life.
>
> As life in primitive societies revolves around the weather, what you're looking to Baal for is the right mix of sun and rain to guarantee the harvest.[2]

Elijah, whose name is variously translated, 'The real God is Yahweh' or 'The Lord is my God' watches in the wings, waits for God's time, then strikes. Appearing out of the blue, like a well-aimed arrow, he heads straight for his target, King Ahab, and makes this fearless God-inbreathed claim: 'In the name of the LORD, the living God of Israel, whom I serve, I tell you that there will be no dew or rain for the next two or three years until I say so' (1 Kings 17:1 GNB).

Just that. His one short, pithy prophecy safely delivered, he returns to the obscurity of the desert. He retreats at the command of God: 'Leave here, turn eastward and hide in the Kerith Ravine, east of the Jordan. You will drink from the brook, and I have ordered the ravens to feed you there' (1 Kings 17:3,4).

The desert – a place of hiddenness

God sends Elijah into the desert to hide him from the wrath of Jezebel. God knows that Jezebel will be infuriated by Elijah's prophecy; that she will recognize that the forthcoming drought is a sign of God's judgement on a nation that has so wantonly disobeyed and forsaken him. She knows, too, that Elijah is publicly challenging the popular belief that Baal is not only the fertility god but also the lord of the rain clouds. God knows the ruthless Jezebel will set up a witch-hunt for Elijah – leaving no stone unturned until he is found and killed. God must therefore hide and protect his servant. His public ministry is not yet finished; it has only just begun.

God has another reason for concealing Elijah. If the prophet is to be effective for him, he needs the refining and the empowering that is the desert's gift to us. Albert Osborn puts this well: 'Before speaking publicly about God, we ought always to be sure that God's Word is in our very bones, burning for expression. Thousands of our words will not equal a few of God's words.'[3]

Elijah is to publicly challenge the tenets of Baal. Before he does this, Yahweh's promise must 'burn for expression' in his heart: 'If you follow my decrees and are careful to obey my commands, I will send you rain in its season, and the ground will yield its crops' (Leviticus 26:3).[4]

Watch Elijah, then, wend his way through one thicket after another, through one narrow pass after another, to a narrow glen overhung with a tangled wood where a brook gurgles its way between the gaunt, rocky masses. There in this gorge – God's hiding place – he sits camouflaged by his hairy cloak that blends so beautifully with the colour of the cave. Listen to the silence that enshrouds this place – a silence that is disturbed only by the cry of the solitary bittern, the raucous racket made by the ravens, the occasional hissing of a snake, the distant roar of a lion or two, the incessant chuckle of the brook, the still, small, voice of God – and his own reflections.

What are Elijah's thoughts and feelings here in the hiddenness? Does he sometimes feel full of frustration as he thinks of Ahab's blatant disobedience, Jezebel's ruthlessness, the

Ravens in the Jordan Valley

apostasy of his people and their need of a leader? Is he champing at the bit, desperate to return to rescue the nation from the current crisis? Does he feel jealous of the prophets who have not been forced to flee? Does he feel de-skilled, forgotten, over-looked, worthless, shunted into a siding? Does he sometimes cry out, like the psalmist, 'How long, O LORD?'

Or does he relish the silence? As he sits and strolls, as he gazes and beholds, as he listens and learns, as he marvels at the regular meals delivered to him by the ravens, does his heart thrill to the language of creation? Do the towering rocks speak of God's greatness and his own littleness – of God's grandeur and his own ordinariness? Does the solid mass of rock with its countless nooks and crannies and protective caves testify to the protective part of God's nature that provides shelter, not only from enemies like Jezebel but from the relentless glare of the Middle Eastern sun? Does he learn to 'read God's other book', the book of nature, as he examines every petal and sepal of each tiny opening spring flower: crocuses, anemones, wild cyclamen, miniature irises and narcissi that appear, as from nowhere, in this part of the world?

Does the vastness and the brightness of the night sky fill him with awe and wonder: the inky blackness of it with its myriad of stars and its sometimes cheese-coloured, sometimes blood-orange moon so clearly seen in this place where no other lights vie for attention? Does he take time to contemplate every bubble and droplet of the brook? Does he tune into the music of the flowing stream? Does he contemplate the crags of the granite walls, the lichen that grows on its great, grotesque face as well as in its cracks and crannies, the towering, poker-straight pine trees, the play of the sun on the sometimes friendly, sometimes frowning forests? Does he relish the pure, unpolluted nectar God provides for his sustenance – water from the stream? Does he befriend every pine cone, become acquainted with every butterfly, study the spaces between things – like the gentian sky peeping between the evergreens? Do the shapes of the rocks and shrubs and pieces of bark intrigue him? Does the texture of the water and the pine needles, the birds' feathers and the insect wings delight him? Do the colours of God's world soothe his soul: the brown of the parched earth, the unbroken blue of the sky, the greens of the forest, the buffs and blondes of the grasses, the greys of the granite rocks, the mauves and lilacs, creams and pinks, lemons and paper-whites of the wild flowers and butterflies? Does he find himself lost in wonder, love and praise as he sits musing outside his cave, alone, watching the silvery light of a full moon transform the grotto he now calls home? Possibly. As James reminds us, Elijah 'was a man just like us' (5:17). In silence, away from the noise and the pressures, the frustrations and tough questions life poses, we see more clearly, understand more fully, and hear more distinctly. Stillness is the school all would-be listeners to God must attend for a long, long time if they would learn the art and enjoy the privilege of focused listening and focused loving.

Sometimes this silence is alive – full of the chatter of birds, the rustling of the wind through the trees, the urgent hum of bees and the discernible still, small voice of God At other times it is the powerful kind of silence David Runcorn experienced:

> The intensity was alarming. There was an almost physical quality to it. It pressed upon me like the heat of the sun above . . . Like an uncompromising but faithful companion, [it] pursued me, questioning, probing, seeking truth. . . . At other times, in the early morning or in the evening, the silence softened and yielded in a stillness that wove its presence round me like a seamless robe. There seemed to be no part of life that it didn't touch and influence.[5]

The desert – a place of temptation

Camping there, month in and month out, like most desert dwellers, Elijah lurches from one extreme to the other: from the quiet ecstasy of knowing himself drawn by the gravitational pull of God's love to the boredom with it all that André Louf describes so well:

> Solitude is an easy thing only for the beginner who is still thoroughly sick and tired of the noise and pressure of the modern world which he has just recently left. But the desert is not only a place of relaxation, even if God is being sought there. In next to no time it begins to weigh like lead. It can engender boredom. And one gets fed up with it. It fairly quickly presents itself as both inhospitable and uninhabitable. The moment comes for every recluse when he finds himself on the point of running away from solitude and giving up prayer. This is the hardest moment, on which everything depends, the classic temptation of accidie, boredom, dreariness. This temptation we can only withstand in the power of the Spirit . . .[6]

Is Elijah tempted to run away? This temptation surely tugs at him from the first day onwards? After all, he's been brought up to believe that ravens are to be avoided at all costs. Had not God decreed: 'These are the birds you are to detest and not eat because they are detestable: the eagle, the vulture . . . any kind of raven' (Leviticus 11:13,15 cf Deuteronomy 14:14).

Ravens feed on carrion, offal and on rotting matter. Yet God clearly said that the birds that would feed him are these creatures Elijah would dismiss as repulsive. Does Elijah feel nauseous as, morning by morning and night by night, ravens carry in their big, soiled beaks meat and bread, meat and more bread, more meat and yet more bread? Does prejudice against these 'detestable birds' tempt Elijah to run away? Does the unvaried diet add fuel to the flames of temptation? Does he panic as he watches that energetic, laughing, frothing stream turn into a trickle and then become a mere puddle whose meagre water supply is greedily sucked up by the sun? Does fear that he is being condemned to die a slow, lingering death tempt him to leave his hideaway prematurely? Does the very isolation of his hiding place become increasingly irksome as the weeks become long, lonely months? Does loneliness prompt him to flee? Quite possibly – particularly on long, cold winter nights when clouds hide the moon and stars and he sits and stares into a space of total darkness. 'Elijah was a man just like us.'

If such temptations come, Elijah resists them. In doing so, the desert becomes the chisel with which the Creator re-shapes and re-moulds his servant.

As each temptation is confronted and rejected, Elijah becomes more and more like the trees in the forest that frame his cave: slowly but surely he pushes strong, sturdy, tenacious roots of trust down and out until the part of him that is not seen, his inner self, grows as healthy as his outer self. Unable to fend for himself in any way, he abandons himself to God and discovers him to be the Trustworthy One. As he trusts, he learns lessons that he needs to learn experientially – to acknowledge his own nothingness, his own poverty, his own defencelessness, his own limitations, his own need of help. Consequently, he learns to allow God to be God, he learns to listen and to wait. Eventually, these lessons learned, Elijah hears God's voice: 'Go at once to Zarephath . . . and stay there. I have commanded a widow in that place to supply you with food' (1 Kings 17:9).

The desert – a place of miracles
Elijah goes. Does he leave readily or reluctantly? We are not told.

Neither are we told what thoughts fill his mind as he walks the seventy-three miles north to Zarephath in present-day Lebanon. We are told that 'Zarephath' means 'a smelter's crucible'. In this crucible, God's prophet is to be further changed. Stripped now of all resources, Elijah ventures into another kind of desert – the desert of dependency. The prophet who is renowned for so fearlessly confronting Ahab emerges from his hiding place with nothing to give, nothing to say. Unable to offer the widow anything, he can only hold out empty hands and beg. What is more, he, an Israelite, is forced to depend on a Lebanese woman – a Gentile. In this humiliating moment, he discovers that the prophetic gift has not died; it is as pertinent and powerful as ever: 'The jar of flour will not be used up and the jug of oil will not run dry until the day the LORD gives rain on the land,' he promises the widow (1 Kings 17:14).

Is he gratified when she believes him – even perceives that he is a 'man of God'?

How humiliating, then, to watch the widow's son fall ill, lie languishing and then die. Elijah knows what to do. Taking the child from his mother's arms, he carries him to his 'prophet's chamber' and, movingly, stretches himself on the Gentile boy's body – despite Numbers 19:16: 'Anyone out in the open who touches someone who has been killed with a sword or someone who has died a natural death, or anyone who touches a human bone or a grave, will be unclean for seven days.'

His prayer is desperate, urgent, bold, to the point: 'Let this boy's life return to him!' (1 Kings 17:21), he cries three times. 'The boy's life returned to him, and he lived' (v 22). Like many other desert dwellers before and since, Elijah learns that the desert is the place where God delights to do miracles. And what a miracle! As Lance Pierson observes:

This is the first resurrection in the Bible. Elijah was asking

God to do something new. There is good reason to think
that God gave Elijah assurance that he was praying in the
right direction. His prayer outreaches his earlier
experience. It is the stretching of faith to cross frontiers, to
conquer new territory and occupy it for God. He prayed
big and complimented God.[7]

Surely, Elijah is ready now for the challenges ahead? 'Not yet',
God says. 'After a long time, in the third year, the word of the
LORD came to Elijah: "Go" ' (1 Kings 18:1).

'After a long time. . . .' Does Elijah grow tired or resentful of
the waiting? Or does he realise that when we wait, we allow God
to be God? Does he realise that, 'effective work for God takes
years of preparation.'[8] Does he realise that God is purifying and
refining him in the crucible, that God will not permit him to
emerge from that crucible prematurely because, if he is removed
too soon, he will remain immature, incomplete, malformed?
Instead of removing his prophet from the furnace, God gives
him the grace to stay until the moment is ripe: for him and for
the nation. Does he realise how, in the hiddenness of Kerith, his
ability to hear God has been sharpened, that he has been further
filled with the very fullness of God. God speaks through him and
God's healing power now flows through the prophet. Does he
realise that the accolades are given to Elijah rather than to God?

Does pride wriggle into his soul? Is that why God kept him
in Zarephath for so long? Possibly. 'He was a man like us' and we
find it so easy, when God uses us, to pat *ourselves* on the back, to
congratulate *ourselves*, to assume that we have arrived spiritually.
We find it so easy to forget to give the glory to God. We may pay
lip-service to God's part in the miracle but, in the secret places of
our hearts, pride finds a niche.

Could it be that pride is one of Elijah's weaknesses? Do we
find a hint of this in the rather arrogant prayer that he prays

when begging God to restore life to the dead little Lebanese boy? Is he not here, in effect, berating God, asking him: 'What are you playing at, God?': 'O LORD my God, have you brought tragedy also upon this widow I am staying with, by causing her son to die?' (1 Kings 17:20).

Was he wanting God to resuscitate the child for the child's sake, the mother's sake, to save his own face – or a mixture of all three?

Are we to catch another glimpse of this same tendency to self-aggrandisement when Elijah climbs Mount Carmel and boasts: 'I am the only one of the LORD's prophets left, but Baal has four hundred and fifty prophets' (18:22)? (A twice-repeated boast that echoes round the cave on Mount Horeb.)[9]

Does God keep his prophet in the smelting furnace of Zarephath until humility becomes part of the warp and woof of his life? 'We learn humility from pondering the vast chasm that lies between us, our fallen desires and our habits on the one hand and God's purpose for our life on the other.'[10] When humility becomes a part of us, when things go well, we take a little bit of encouragement for ourselves but give all the glory to God.

Or does God continue to keep Elijah in the furnace until he is purified and refined from other 'besetting sins' – until he is ready to be further empowered by God for the unenviable challenge that lies just around the corner?

We are not told. Neither are we told whether Elijah was content to wait or resentful. What we are told is that 'after a long time, in the third year [of the drought], the word of the LORD came to Elijah: "Go and present yourself to Ahab, and I will send rain on the land" ' (18:1). Elijah goes.

The desert – a place of over-stimulation
There are many kinds of desert: the deserts like Kerith where, in the stillness, we know ourselves loved, not for anything we have

done nor for anything we can do but because of who we are. There are deserts like Zarephath where, as we interact with others, our own imperfections rise to the surface and demand to be dealt with: where we are purged and purified before we are empowered. And there is the desert of over-stimulation where events insist that we act and react rather than reflect; where we are bombarded with words, expectations (other people's and our own) and challenges – maybe with conflict. Perhaps the desert of over-stimulation is the most difficult to negotiate – at least for some personality types. Perhaps it is the most dangerous to the soul because it often feels like fulfilment or success rather than the resourcelessness and lostness that it very often is.

God now sends Elijah into this desert of over-stimulation. No rain has fallen for three years. Drought has given rise to severe famine. The situation is so desperate that Ahab, the king, and Obadiah, the faithful prophet of God, scour the land, visiting personally every spring and valley in search of enough blades of grass to keep their horses and mules alive. Failure to find fodder will necessitate a mass slaughter of their livestock. Elijah learns this news from Obadiah. He also learns that, while he has been in hiding, Ahab has had every nation and kingdom searched in the hope of unearthing Elijah's whereabouts and Jezebel has massacred God's prophets. As though this was not enough, Ahab accuses him of being 'the troubler of Israel'.

Ahab's accusations trigger Elijah's righteous rage. Springing into action, he masterminds 'the epic of Mount Carmel',[11] wins a landslide victory for God through his prayer, massacres 850 prophets of Baal and Asherah, releases rain, races miles through a cloud burst – and then collapses in a heap in the terrifying desert of fear, perceived failure and despair where he begs God to take away his life, complaining bitterly, 'I have had enough' (19:4).

The desert – a place of despair

No one can even begin to assess how fast the adrenalin flowed as Elijah made his way to Ahab's palace, what it cost him to mount the massive, public demonstration of God's power on Mount Carmel and to order and oversee the murder of nearly one thousand men. A man of his temperament who survived, even thrived on three years of solitude can project extraversion, can cope magnificently while doing so, but at very great cost to himself. He then needs reassurance and affirmation. If, after being over-stretched in this way, he is condemned rather than applauded, he is in danger of collapsing because, in order to operate in this extravert way, he has to don a mask, a persona – that front we put on when we prepare to meet people and relate to the world. As John Sanford explains:

> The persona has a double function. One function is to help us project our personality effectively into the world. The other function is to protect us from the outer world by enabling us to assume a certain outer posture but at the same time keep other aspects of ourselves hidden from others. The persona is often useful and necessary. It enables us to be effective in our dealings with the world, but also to protect ourselves when that is necessary.[12]

Although the persona is therefore invaluable, there are certain dangers inherent in relying on it for too long. When we resort to functioning frequently through the persona and when the persona is so far removed from the genuine personality that it camouflages the person we really are, then a serious problem occurs – an inevitable energy loss. When we are being genuine, on the other hand, our energy level is topped up.[13] As James Houston sums up the situation, 'the bigger we grow, the less authentic we become'.[14]

Energy seeped, then poured, from Elijah as he worked for and won that super-human victory for and in the name of God. Consequently, when confronted by Jezebel, like an inflated balloon that has been deliberately slashed, he collapsed – not physically, at first. The physical collapse happened after he had put some 120 miles between himself and Jezebel. It was preceded by an emotional nose-dive into the abyss of despair, desolation and self-rejection: 'He came to a broom tree, sat down under it and prayed that he might die. "I have had enough, LORD," he said. Take my life; I am no better than my ancestors" ' (19:4).

God, the God of the desert, the Tender One, who wooed Elijah into the desert in the first place does not abandon his 'suicidal saint'.[15] He guides the exhausted prophet's faltering footsteps to that tree that is so attractive to the desert dweller: the broom tree. Was it covered with its white, perfumed blossom? Did its fragrance fill the evening air? Did its silver-grey branches fan Elijah's feverish face as, thankfully, he curled up in its shade? We are not told. We are told that God's weary one sank into a long, deep, much-needed, refreshing, God-given sleep. We are also told, by implication, that God was watching, caring and acting on Elijah's behalf. No rowdy ravens now carry him food. They are replaced by God's own angel who cooks fresh bread for him, and waits on him, personally providing water as well as food.

Does this angel suggest to Elijah that he journeys on to 'the mountain of God', Mount Horeb? Or was Elijah already en route for 'the mountain of Moses', as Mount Horeb was popularly known? Again, we are not told. We are told that it took him forty days and forty nights to make this arduous trip – the Bible's way of indicating that it took a 'very long time'.

Away from the limelight, away from the razzmatazz, strangely strengthened physically by the God-given sustenance, amid some of the most spectacular scenery in the world, Elijah, at last, processes the rebel emotions that have given birth to that soul-destroying death wish. The desert is the place where we can give vent to our seething emotions and, having poured them out, not to a sea of sand, but to the God who cares, to expose the hurt that gives rise to the rage. Here, in possibly the self-same cave where Moses met with God, Elijah rails at his Creator: 'I feel you've let me down', he hints. '*I've* been really zealous for you because your people have rejected you but *you* . . .'

The anger no longer swirls around inside him. The volcano has erupted. The molten lava pours down the mountainside. 'I'm lonely,' Elijah continues. 'I'm the only one left. All the others have either turned apostate or been butchered to death. And I'm terrified. They're determined to kill me now.'

God does not retaliate. He metes out no recriminations, no rebukes, no remonstrances. Instead, he offers his servant concentrated listening and focussed love followed by one measured piece of wise, compassionate counsel, 'Go out, stand on the mountain in my presence'.

Does Elijah recall that it was on this very spot that God had said to Moses, 'There is a place near me where you may stand on a rock' (Exodus 33:21)? Does he recall that it was said of Moses, 'The LORD would speak to Moses face to face, as a man speaks with his friend' (Exodus 33:11)? Did such memories give a glimmer of hope? If so, how does he feel when, for days, maybe weeks, he experiences the seeming absence of God rather than his promised presence? How does he feel as he watches the terrifying tornado rip the mountains apart, shattering and hurling stones as it rages round the holy mount? How does he feel as the foundations beneath his feet shudder and shake and threaten to open up and swallow him when the earthquake follows close on the tail of the tornado? How does he feel when even the all-consuming fire, the traditional symbol of God's presence, fails to reveal the Almighty? Do these phenomena

The summit of 'the mountain of Moses'.

confirm his worst fear – that God has indeed absented himself? Does he consequently feel even more embittered, angry, resentful, let down? Possibly. 'He was a man like us' as well as 'a man like Moses'.

The desert is a place where God appears to abandon us, where his apparent absence confuses and distresses us. It confuses us because, having served him faithfully, we feel he owes us a reward. Like petulant children, when no reward appears, or when the desired reward fails to appear, we feel peeved. It distresses us because, deep down, we know that God is our pearl of great price. For his sake we would sell everything. Life without him is no life at all. Our hearts long for him, cry out for him, yearn for him. When he returns, we respond to his faintest whisper – like Elijah.

The tornado blows itself out, the earthquake stops, the fire dies and a deafening silence holds Mount Horeb in its grip – that holy, hushed kind of silence that stops you in your tracks, that almost makes your heart miss a beat, that prompts you to hold your breath lest you should pollute it with sound. Into that profound silence, God drops his earlier question: 'What are you doing here?'

'What are you doing here, Elijah, in this holy place so sacred to Moses, so sacred to me; this place where Moses' face shone as he radiated My glory?'

The desert of despair is the place where we watch one action replay after another of those grievances we accuse of causing our collapse. The desert of despair is also the place where God smiles on us, presses the pause button, gives short-term, manageable goals, reveals that feelings and facts do not necessarily coincide and re-commissions and enlightens the 'honourably wounded'.[16]

'Whose kingdom are you serving?' he seems gently to ask his servant. 'The kingdom of Elijah or the kingdom of God? I know that you desire to restore the Law of Moses, but like Moses before you who also nearly collapsed, you need help. Help is at hand,' God seems to insist. 'Start by going and enlisting the support of Hazael, Nimshi and Elisha. And, by the way, you're not the only one left': "I reserve seven thousand in Israel – all whose knees have not bowed down to Baal and all whose mouths have not kissed him." '[17]

As always, Elijah obeyed. Like other giants of the faith, he emerged from the desert empowered and with a renewed vision.

When, just before his disappearance into heaven (2 Kings 2:1 ff), his cloak fell, physically and symbolically, on Elisha, 'fifty men of the company of the prophets watched' (2 Kings 2:7). Had Elijah become the Principal of the School of the Prophets? If so, was he the first teacher of desert spirituality? We can only surmise. What we can be sure of, however, is that Elijah's prophetic ministry continued to cut ice as effectively after his breakdown as before it. Even his mission to Ahab bore fruit. After Ahab had incurred the wrath of God yet again, Elijah confronts him yet again. The result was startling. As God put it to his prophet: 'Have you noticed how Ahab has humbled himself before me? Because he has humbled himself, I will not bring this disaster in his day, but I will bring it on his house in the days of his son' (1 Kings 21:29).

We can also be sure that, if we are serious about following Christ, we, too, will be led into the desert. James Houston puts the situation well:

> There is not one kind of desert experience, but as many as there are differing personalities and personal stories, yours and mine.
>
> For the 'perfectionist' there is the desert of imperfection, where we have to face up to our own weaknesses and let God alone give us the humility to face and work through them. For the 'giver' there is the desert of inadequacy, where we face the flight from our own sinfulness. We too are in need of help from others and, above all, from our God.
>
> The 'doer' is lured into the desert of uselessness where we seem to get nowhere and where we face up to the need to become a powerless 'child' of God. The 'idealist' who has assumed romantically that life will be interpreted and identity given merely by artistic creativity is placed in the

desert of ordinariness. The 'observer' or 'scholar' is placed in the desert of solitude until the inner loneliness that substituted 'ideas' for relationships has been confronted . . .

The 'rigid' or 'loyal' maintainer of the *status quo*, afraid of change, is placed in a desert of flux that appears as disorienting as sand flying in the desert winds. The 'fun-lover' who fears suffering and pain will wander in the desert of desolation, where for a time life is dominated by pain. Similarly, the 'controller' ends up in the desert of weakness, and is made vulnerable to the threat of the chaotic in a wholly new way. The 'pleaser' or 'peace-maker' needs freedom in the desert storms where survival requires confrontation with reality, and refuge lies only in God – learning to speak the truth becomes a terrible risk that has to be taken.[18]

In the light of this challenging claim, maybe the story of Elijah's sojourns in the wilderness challenges us to ask, 'Which of the deserts mentioned in this chapter have I encountered? How did God use this particular desert experience to transform or re-mould me?'

FIVE

Four Female Desert-Dwellers:

The widow of Zarephath, Sarah, Miriam and Mary

Each of the four heroes of the faith we have focussed on had a female companion for at least part of their desert journey. So the last chapter could have been called 'Elijah and the widow of Zarephath'. Chapter three could have been called 'Moses and Miriam'. 'Abraham and Sarah' and 'Jesus and Mary' would, perhaps, have been better headings for chapters two and one respectively. In a patriarchal society like the Middle East, however, men assume the centre stage far more frequently than women. That is why more is written about men than their female counterparts. Yet the four women concerned were all transformed in desert-like terrain that has a contemporary ring about it. None of their stories are 'they lived happily ever after' fairy tales. They are horrifyingly real and relevant to today's men and women of faith. It seems appropriate, therefore, that a cameo of each of these women should contribute to 'the last word'.

The widow of Zarephath

When the curtain rises on the widow of Zarephath, her clothing and her body language betray her. She's dressed in black and she's gathering fuel for her final fire. In other words, she's racked with pain.

Life was tough for widows in Old Testament times. It was tough legally because, in the absence of insurance policies, the welfare state or the equivalent – a male protector – a widow was always in danger of abuse and exploitation. The Mosaic Law recognised this: 'Do not take advantage of a widow or an orphan. If you do and they cry out to me, I will certainly hear their cry. My anger will be aroused, and I will kill you with the sword; your wives will become widows . . .' (Exodus 22:22).

Even so, a widow left without children or with only young children, found it hard to survive. Life was tough practically, too, because without a male relative, widows were left to fend for themselves. God made provision for *Israelite* widows in a number of ways. At harvest time, grain was to be left in the fields, olives were to be left on the trees and grapes on the vine so that the poor could gather sufficient to eat. (The 'poor' included widows, orphans and unemployed foreigners.[1]) Every third year, additional provision was to be made: 'When you have finished setting aside a tenth of all your produce in the third year, the year of the tithe, you shall give it to . . . the widow, so that they may eat in your towns and be satisfied' (Deuteronomy 26:12).

And every seventh year the land was to enjoy a Sabbath. It was to be left uncultivated, vines and trees unpruned so that 'the poor among your people may get food from it' (Exodus 23:10).

But these laws applied to the Israelites, and the widow of Zarephath lived in the heart of Baal country where she was protected by no such laws. So we find her gathering, not the

Death in the desert.

customary bundle of kindling and firewood which would need to be carried home on her back but just 'a few sticks to take home and make a meal for myself and my son, that we may eat it – and die' (1 Kings 17:12).

In other words, this woman, like thousands of people in the two-thirds world today, stared starvation in the face. Her resources had all but run out. She was not only impoverished, she was hurting emotionally. The popular belief that widowhood was a reproach from God made certain of that. This belief insisted that the woman or her relatives must have sinned grievously to have earned from God a punishment as severe as widowhood. The kind of cruel question was often asked of a widow that the disciples asked of the man born blind: 'Who sinned? This man or his parents ...?'(John 9:2–3).

Widows consequently suffered untold humiliation, shame and guilt – in addition to the shock, heartache, ongoing loneliness and grief, and the sense of emptiness and loss that is part of the normal grief process.

What was this widow thinking that morning when Elijah walked purposefully through Zarephath's town gate and asked her for a drink of water (1 Kings 17:10)? Was she weary with worry? Was she bleary-eyed from lack of sleep? Did unanswerable questions tumble round her mind: 'What will happen to us?'; 'Why me?'; 'What have I done to deserve this?'; 'Why is there so much suffering in the world?'

We are not told. Neither are we told whether or not this woman was a believer. Maybe she was? Maybe this was why God chose her to feed Elijah? Maybe this was how she recognised him as a man of God? Maybe this was why she didn't protest unduly when Elijah made the seemingly selfish and inappropriate request that, before making a final meal for herself and her son, she should first make a cake of bread for him? Maybe this was the reason why she believed Elijah's strange prophecy: 'Don't be afraid . . . The jar of flour will not be used up and the jug of oil will not run dry until the day the LORD gives rain on the land' (1 Kings 17:13,14)?

Whether she was a believer or simply a pagan woman who recognised Elijah as a prophet because of his dress and, possibly, the demeanour of this man who had spent a whole year in solitude, she was clearly someone on whom the hand of God rested. She did as God had instructed – and more – she fed Elijah and gave him a home in the 'upper room', probably the guest room on the flat roof of her house.[2]

The desert – the place where miracles happen

Her reward was startling and moving. At the height of the drought with its consequent famine, while others were dying of starvation, in her household 'there was food every day . . . For the jar of flour was not used up and the jug of oil did not run dry . . .' (1 Kings 17:15,16).

Were there other rewards? Did Elijah's presence above her home bring her a sense of security, of shalom, of 'kinship'?

> Kinship is a rich bondedness that calls forth to the deepest part of ourselves. It is a mutuality of understanding, a sense of belonging, a union of spirits, a loving apprecia-tion and a deep communion which comes from having known experiences similar to the person with whom we are bonded. Kinship . . . encourages us to 'hang in there' when the going gets particularly difficult or over-whelming.[3]

Was she able to air some of her unanswerable questions with Elijah? Was she conscious of his prayers for herself and her son? Was she, consequently, beginning to soften in the middle of her sorrow? Did her home gradually feel more like an oasis than the desert? Possibly. A listening ear and a caring presence is to the love-hungry heart what water is to cracked, parched earth. Imagine her, like a crushed though not broken desert flower that is slowly opening its petals once more. Imagine, then, the shock, the sorrow and the shame crushing her once more as first she watches her son fall sick, then she watches him fighting for his life and finally she watches as death steals him from her.

The extent of her wrath betrays the extent of the trust she had begun to place in Elijah. Anger is a secondary emotion. Underneath anger lies another, stronger emotion – hurt, fear or rejection. And the widow of Zarephath is now very, very hurt. At this moment in time, she is unable or unwilling to unveil the hurt. Instead, she gives vent to her rage: 'What do you have against me, man of God? Did you come to remind me of my sin and kill my son?' (1 Kings 17:18).

What happens to the anger and the hurt as she watches Elijah scoop up the body of her son? Does she follow him to the upper room? Does she sense the prophet's distress and concern? Does she eavesdrop on his desperate prayer: 'O LORD my God, let this boy's life return to him!'? Or does she stay downstairs – too absorbed in her own grief and worry and weeping to notice what Elijah is doing? After all, she has now re-entered the desert of loss with a vengeance. She has now lost the most precious person in her life – precious, not simply because of who he is but also because of what he represents – her security for the future. She has now lost what might have been. Her son, had he come of age, would have inherited the house. She would have lived there with him until she died. Her future would have been secure. Now that he is dead, the house must revert immediately to her husband's family. What will become of her? Who will look after her in her old age? Why did God provide them with food to keep them alive only to play this cruel trick on them? Will her past failure haunt her forever? Such questions fan the flame of her inconsolable grief – until Elijah emerges from the upper room, still carrying her child. The child God has brought back from the dead!

What does she do when she sees him and hears him and holds his warm body in her own arms? How does she respond to Elijah's: 'Look, your son is alive!' (v 23)?

We are not told. We are told that she insists: 'Now I know . . .' (v 24).

As the curtain falls, we bid farewell to a changed woman: knowing that Elijah is a man of God, certain that he really is God's mouth-piece, confident that God's word is trustworthy and true. Do we also leave her knowing 'the Lord' (v 24) for herself? Or searching for a relationship with him? Does she, at least, know that the God who allowed her son to die and who allowed her to suffer, suffered with her? Has she seen God's suffering reflected in the mirror of Elijah's eyes and face? Again, we are not told. We are told that Elijah remained in Zarephath for 'a long time' – to be served by a hostess who still has problems – she is still a widow – but a hostess who has been truly transformed by the desert of loss; a hostess who is now at peace in her pain.

Before moving on, there would be value in pausing to reflect on the experiences of the widow of Zarephath and to ask ourselves whether her story finds any parallels in our own life by asking:

- Have I ever been knocked sideways by the unexpected?
- Have I ever been becalmed by loss?
- If so, who met me in this desert place?
- What happened as a result?

Sarah

Sarah spent most of her life in the desert – not simply wandering here and there in a sea of sand but drowning in a sea of sadness also. A single sentence sums up her pain: 'Now Sarai was barren; she had no children' (Genesis 11:30).

Untold suffering lurks in that succinct statement. The inability to bear children not only deprived a couple of the personal happiness and pride Middle Easterners derive from their off-spring, it denied them a much-longed-for heir. Worse, childlessness carried a stigma. Popular belief insisted that barrenness was a sign of God's displeasure. So we find the infertile Hannah pleading with God for a child out of 'great anguish and grief' (1 Samuel 1:10). Likewise, we find Elizabeth – and Rachel before her (Genesis 30:23) – rejoicing in the miraculous birth of her son, not least because, as a result of the birth, 'The Lord has . . . taken away my disgrace among the people' (Luke 1:25).

Sarah was not only the victim of public shame and public blame, she suffered privately and she suffered often. She lived in a society where women did not go out to work. They spent a great deal of time socialising, talking 'women's talk' with their children in tow. When the conversation centred round the children, did Sarah feel on the fringe, worthless, isolated, lonely, hurting, despised? Probably. These are words women in her position often use to describe the emotions they wrestle with on such occasions. Did the well of inner grief fill up at such times – the grief of what might have been if only God had 'opened her womb'?

Add to this pain the regular onset of her monthly period – that physical phenomenon that seems to mock the would-be mother – and her husband's obvious and frequently expressed dismay that she had not given him a son, and we piece together a picture of a very unhappy person. Outwardly Sarah was a woman of outstanding and enviable beauty (Genesis 12:11,14), inwardly she was becoming increasingly vulnerable and fragile as those damaging messages from the past echoed round her heart: 'You're useless, you're not wanted'.

The desert – the place where we become more self-aware

Victor Frankl, a psychotherapist who suffered but survived the atrocities and indignities of the Nazi concentration camp in Auschwitz claims that personal pain confronts us with a personal choice. Commenting on this claim, Joyce Rupp suggests:

> We can respond [to pain] with anger and bitterness by being stoical and not allowing ourselves to cry or to have anyone comfort us. We can be the martyr, full of self-pity, bemoaning our pain forever and becoming self-centred. We can give up, let ourselves stay depressed, stop trying to put life into our life, or we can gradually grow wiser and find deeper meaning in our existence.[4]

Sarah, it seems, chose to respond to her day-in day-out burden with understandable rage, bitterness, self-pity and self-absorption. Without a mentor or friend to hear her pain, mirror to her her worth or express ongoing care, the pain became intolerable. And Abram, it appears, contributed to the problem. When he heard and responded to God's call to leave Ur, for example, we simply read: 'He took his wife Sarai . . . and they set out for the land of Canaan' (Genesis 12:5).

Sarah would not have expected her husband to consult her, of course. Neither would she have expected him to make a distinction between her, his possessions and his slaves. She knew that, in society's eyes, she was a mere chattel. Statusless. But even a statusless refugee has feelings. We are not told how Sarah felt about being uprooted from her home in Ur, how she felt about exchanging the luxuries and conveniences of the city for the hardships of the desert. Middle Eastern women, then as now, love colour and beauty, fine clothes and jewellery – and perfume. Did Sarah sometimes drown her sorrows in such distractions while she lived in the city? If so, as she waded through wave after wave of restless sand and journeyed through arid wastes and flint-studded hillsides, did she find the desert irksome, bland and empty? Did the sweltering heat and the blistering sun in this land that was devoid of human habitation only intensify her loneliness and sorrow? Was this why her bitterness took root?

We don't know. Neither do we know how she felt about that back-handed compliment Abraham gave her as they approached Egypt:

> He said to his wife Sarai, 'I know what a beautiful woman you are. When the Egyptians see you, they will say, "This is his wife." Then they will kill me but will let you live. Say you are my sister, so that I will be treated well for your sake and my life will be spared because of you.'[5]

Did Abraham *have* to implicate Sarah in his deception? Did he *have* to force her into further suffering so that life would be easier for him? Could he not see that this would humiliate her even further and plunge her into even deeper sorrow? Did self so fill his horizon that he saw but didn't care? Is that how Sarah read the situation? Again, we don't know. We do know that, eventually, the boil of bitterness burst and the pus of hopelessness and despair poured out of it. To make matters worse God, it must have seemed to the now-desperate Sarah, was consistently rubbing salt in her heart-wound by promising Abraham that he would sire nations: 'Look up at the heavens and count the stars. . . . So shall your offspring be' (Genesis 15:5).

'Abram believed' – but ten whole agonising years later, Sarah still smarted from the stigma of 'barrenness'. Believing that God had failed to keep his promise and acting culturally correctly, in her desperation, Sarah suggested that Abraham should 'go, sleep with my maidservant; perhaps I can build a family through her' (Genesis 16:2).

The desert – a place where God remains in control

'Perhaps I can build a family through her.' A statement as heavy with sorrow and desperation as this one flows from an inner wound that will not stop bleeding. The ploy was doomed to failure. Few women can tolerate a perceived rival to her husband's affections without screaming inwardly and irrationally from the seeming rejection and betrayal – not even when the harem is the accepted norm. Hagar's attitude to her mistress was almost the last straw. Was it Hagar's pride because she was pregnant while her mistress remained barren that riled Sarah or was it Abraham's undisguised delight that, at long last, he was to be a father, that hurt her so deeply? We don't know. We do know that Sarah's rage now knows no bounds. Unleashing it, she rounds on Abraham, accusing him and blaming him: 'You are responsible for the wrong I am suffering.' And she ill-treats Hagar until, eventually, Hagar flees.

Hating, hurting, irrational though she is, God doesn't give up on her. The desert is the place where he remains firmly in control.

The God who allowed Sarah to remain childless for his own perfect purposes, the God who wooed her husband into the wilderness, is the God who is not knocked off balance by our inability to handle the pain he permits.

While Sarah is still hopelessly lost in the desert of despair, he makes another solemn promise to Abraham: 'I will bless [Sarah] and will surely give you a son *by her*. I will bless her so that she will be the mother of nations; kings of peoples will come from her' (17:15, emphasis mine).

By changing her name from Sarai to Sarah, both of which mean 'Princess', God reminds her that she is not forgotten, not redundant, not worthless. She is uniquely loved. Uniquely his – for naming someone implied ownership. He even makes a *specific* promise – that she would give birth to a son within a year. By this time, however, Sarah has hit the bottom of the pit. Cynicism has set in. She listens to God's promise, laughs a scornful, mocking laugh, then blatantly lies to cover up her cynicism and disbelief. God hears but he doesn't give up on her. He still wants her to become 'the mother of nations'. He still wants the warring couple to be the parents of the new humanity he is bringing into being. He still wants to turn her sorrow into joy. He still wants to take away her shame. And he does. At last, he gives her her heart's desire: a baby boy, born when his mother is in her nineties – a baby whose name, Isaac, means 'laughter'.

The change in Sarah is dramatic: '"God has brought me laughter, and everyone who hears about this will laugh . . . Who would have said to Abraham that Sarah would nurse children? Yet I have borne him a son in his old age"' she cries (Genesis 21:6).

Just as the widow of Zarephath remained a widow even after her son had been raised from the dead, so the legacy of Sarah's desert-like suffering lingers on. Seeing Ishmael, Abraham and Hagar's teenage son, mocking her own son Isaac, Sarah goes on a downward spiral once more. 'While Ishmael lives nearby, he'll always pose a threat to Isaac,' she reasons. Despite the distress her demands cause Abraham, the last words we hear Sarah say are bitter ones: 'Get rid of that slave woman and her son, for that slave woman's son will never share in the inheritance with my

son Isaac' (Genesis 21:10).

Such loaded language! Such on-going bitterness and jealousy and simmering rage! Clearly, Sarah's hurt is not yet healed. Some hurts, particularly the running sore of rejection, take a lifetime to heal. But she's better than she was. She knows now that 'nothing is impossible with God'. She has learned to laugh, learned to marvel and earned an astonishing accolade from the God she has grown to trust. To Abraham God whispers: 'Listen to whatever Sarah tells you, because it is through Isaac that your offspring will be reckoned' (Genesis 21:12).

Thirty years later, when Sarah dies in Hebron, we catch a glimpse of Abraham mourning and weeping at her graveside – weeping for his beautiful 'Princess' whose inner hardness, like a glacier, has melted ever so slightly – enough to turn her frozen rage into rippling laughter. She is still far from perfect. The desert has shown her that. Yet, in the purposes of God, the Sarai who entered the desert was vastly different from the Sarah who has been admitted to the eternal Promised Land before him. When she set out from Ur of the Chaldees she was 'barren', she had no children. Now she is 'the mother of nations' – our mother.

As such, she sets us an example.

What Sarah learned about herself as she journeyed through the desert may not have pleased her, yet she plodded on, refusing to give up. The desert's task is not to delight us but rather to refine us. Even when we don't like it, our task as one present-day desert-dweller puts it, 'is simply to get on with it'.[6] Or, as James Houston reminds us:

For each of us, living the desert experience is a necessary

Sarah's hardness was transformed by the sunshine of God's love.

preparation for walking more closely with God and for being set free . . . to love God more intimately. It is spiritually essential in order to gain more self-knowledge in silence and solitude, so that God's word can penetrate through the different levels of our life's story . . . Patience and gentleness begin to mark our lives more convincingly. The acceptance of suffering is more obvious, it is no longer resentful but even joyous as our spirits rise above the circumstances that constrain us.

It is as if the imprisonment of the desert is essential if we are to win new freedom over all circumstances – if we are to experience the song of the psalmist: 'As they pass through the Valley of Baca [ie weeping], they make it a place of springs' (Psalm 84:6).[7]

Such powerful reminders beg us to pause, to reflect; to ask ourselves some soul-searching questions like:

- Do I want my relationship with God to deepen?
- Am I prepared to journey through a spiritual landscape thatis reminiscent of the bleakness and barrenness of thewilderness?
- Has my spiritual pilgrimage already taken me through desert-like terrain? If so, have I become more self-aware? What did I learn about myself?
- Re-read page 95. Recall occasions when God has had to assure you that you are not forgotten but that you are uniquely loved. How did you respond?

Miriam

From a very early age, it became obvious that Moses' sister, Miriam, would become one of the world's powerful women. Her courage and initiative qualified her for the task of safeguarding her baby brother when he lay hidden in the bulrushes – that courage that prompted her to step forward and ask Pharaoh's daughter: 'Shall I go and get one of the Hebrew women to nurse the baby for you?' (Exodus 2:7).

From what happened subsequently, it seems probable that Moses maintained surreptitious contact with his real family. His link person was almost certainly Miriam. She was known to Moses' foster-mother, the princess, and she was privy to the princess' own secret. Did Miriam also reveal to Moses the secret of his true identity? If so, did she break the news in the presence of the princess? 'The immediate shock of the revelation would otherwise have sent the "prince" scurrying to his "mother" for confirmation.'[8] Was it, perhaps, from Miriam that Moses first learned of the existence of the invisible God the Hebrews worshipped and served? If so, the bonding between brother and sister must have been special and close. How then did Miriam react to Moses' sudden disappearance and the rumours that he had murdered an Egyptian? How did she respond to his return forty years later? We are not told. Neither do we know what she makes of the phenomena that mark Moses' meetings with Pharaoh: 'The Nile is turned to blood; frogs swarm over Egypt; gnats hum; clouds of flies thicken; cattle die; people break out in boils; hail destroys crops and locusts the foliage; darkness enshrouds the Egyptians.'[9]

We do know that she stayed alongside Moses when the Children of Israel watched Pharaoh's horses, chariots and horsemen drown in the Sea of Reeds. In her role as prophetess, she seizes a tambourine and leads all the women in a joyful celebration of the spectacular victory God has just won before their very eyes. Echoing Moses' own song of triumph, she sings to the listening crowd:

> 'Sing to the LORD,
>   for he is highly exalted.
> The horse and its rider
>   he has hurled into the sea.'

(Exodus 15:21)

She and the women then prolong the celebration with dancing and tambourine playing.

We also know that, as time wears on, there in the wilderness she assumes leadership alongside her two brothers: Moses and Aaron. As God puts it to Micah: 'I sent Moses to lead you, also Aaron and Miriam' (Micah 6:4). Or, as the extant, ancient Aramaic translation of that verse puts it, 'I sent Moses to lead the people, Aaron to lead in worship and Miriam to lead the women'. In other words, Miriam enjoys considerable kudos as Moses' and Aaron's sister and as a prophetess in her own right. Such kudos can be lethal to the soul. It panders to the power-hunger from which most of us suffer, it tempts the person in the limelight to promote self rather than, or as well as, God and it gives birth to a jealousy of anyone who threatens to eclipse the one to whom the kudos has been given. Miriam, it seems, fell headlong into this trap.

Her collapse comes at a stressful time for Moses. A deputation arrives from the Children of Israel and starts wailing, 'If only we had meat to eat! We remember the fish we ate in Egypt at no cost – also the cucumbers, melons, leeks, onions and garlic. But now we have lost our appetite; we never see anything but this manna!' (Numbers 11:4–6). 'The rabble' wail so long and so loud that God's anger is aroused prompting a prayer of bitter complaint from Moses:

> 'Why have you brought this trouble on your servant?
> What have I done to displease you that you put the burden
> of all these people on me? Did I conceive all these people?
> Did I give them birth? Why do you tell me to carry them
> in my arms, as a nurse carries an infant, . . .? Where can I
> get meat for all these people? They keep wailing to me,
> 'Give us meat to eat!' I cannot carry all these people by
> myself; the burden is too heavy for me. If this is how you
> are going to treat me, put me to death right now.'
>
> (Numbers 11:11–15)

Hearing Moses' anguish and despair, God draws up a plan to
ensure that help is at hand. Moses is to summon seventy elders
to meet with him and with God.

> So Moses . . . brought together seventy of their elders and
> made them stand round the Tent. Then the LORD came
> down in the cloud and spoke with him, and he took of the
> Spirit that was on him and put the Spirit on the seventy
> elders. When the Spirit rested on them, they prophesied . . .'
>
> (Numbers 11:24–25)

Neither Aaron nor Miriam appear to have been included in this
gathering. Were they jealous of the seventy? Did they feel
threatened by them? Were they resentful of them? If they were,
they said nothing to Moses. Instead, they 'began to talk against
Moses'. The presenting problem about which they publicly
criticise him is 'his Cushite wife'. Is this the real problem? Or is
jealousy of the Spirit-empowering of the seventy the root cause
of their complaint? 'Has the Lord spoken only through Moses?
Hasn't he also spoken through us?' they whine.

Their petulance kindles God's wrath: 'The anger of the Lord burned against [Aaron and Miriam]' (Numbers 12:9). Coming down to meet them in a pillar of cloud, God stands at the Tent, summons and rebukes them. When both Aaron and Miriam step forward, he commands them to listen to his solemn defence of Moses:

> 'When a prophet of the LORD is among you,
>   I reveal myself to him in visions,
>   I speak to him in dreams.
> But this is not true of my servant Moses;
>   he is faithful in all my house.
> With him I speak face to face,
>   clearly and not in riddles;
>   he sees the form of the LORD.
> Why then were you not afraid
>   to speak against my servant Moses?'
>
> (Numbers 12:6–8)

He inflicts on Miriam, the ring-leader, a disfiguring skin disease that makes her an outcast. In response to Moses' desperate plea for healing, God restores her but not before banishing her from the camp for seven days. Because she had sinned publicly, she is forced to suffer the humiliation of a public punishment and because, by criticising Moses, she has defiled herself, she has to pay the statutory price for any kind of uncleanness. Temporary banishment.

Does Miriam ever prophesy again? Does she ever sing or dance or play her tambourine again? Does she ever teach the women again? Probably. God uses the desert to sift us, not to silence us. He sometimes stops us in our tracks and asks pertinent questions: 'Whose kingdom are you serving?'; 'What do you want?' He does this, not to stifle us, but rather to purge

'With [Moses] I speak face to face.'

and purify us.

Miriam failed miserably, but during their long desert pilgrimage, each of God's people failed him in one way or another. The cry, 'Why did you bring us out of Egypt to die in the wilderness?' begins to make itself heard even before the crossing of the Sea of Reeds and recurs with regular monotony throughout the seemingly-endless pilgrimage.

> They fail repeatedly to trust Yahweh, the Lord of the wilderness. They grumble and rebel. They want to go back to Egypt even if it does mean slavery. They cease to want the land God promises. Some of them disobey his orders about the manna, some are seduced by idols.[10]

Each time, though their failure had enraged and saddened him, God had come to them with undeserved love and care: with grace.

As a leader of God's people, a prophetess, Miriam's failure needed a special prescription. Special privileges always go hand in glove with special responsibilities. Does that salutary lesson impress itself on Miriam during those seven days of exile? If so, does it soften her attitude and help to change her attitude to ministry? Does she return to the camp singing a new song encapsulating sentiments like these:

> 'I no longer want to build empires,
> to ascend thrones
> or to be number one in my little kingdom.
> I want to love you,
> and to respond to your love for me
> by communicating such love for others.
> This is what I want, O Lord,
> but you know my soft spots, my hang-ups,

May the victory be yours.'[11]

Or this: 'Lord, turn *my whole being* to your praise and glory.'

Or does she return humbled, chastened, penitent, forgiven, wiser, newly-commissioned?

We are not told. We are told that, over and over again, in this particular wilderness of failure, God's grace triumphs. For,

> when God absolves, it is not a mere amnesty or remission of punishment, but something absolute . . . a total setting free. His forgiveness of our failures re-creates us in his love so that we are as beautiful in his sight as his creative dream would have us. He sees only the lovely things in our lives or perhaps it would be truer to say that he sees our sins and wounds and failures as lovely because transfigured.[12]

We all wander in the wilderness of perceived or actual failure from time to time. that is why we close this chapter with some salutory questions:

- Do I believe that God longs to come to me with constant, unconditional love?
- Do I believe that he uses the desert to sift us, not to silence us?
- Do I believe that, even in the desert of failure, God's grace can and will triumph?

Mary

The desert is the place where men and women encounter God and communicate with him. The desert is also the place where they commune with God, that is, where they enjoy heart-to-heart onenesss with the Holy One, where they are absorbed by him and are caught up with him.

One of the reasons why many Christians envy Jesus' mother is that she was given the privilege of enjoying oneness with God's Son in a unique way.

Take the overwhelming experience of Jesus' gestation, for example, when Mary communed with the child whose heartbeat and kicks and movements she could feel. Or take the oneness that united them as Mary paused to ponder the mystery of the creation of the God-child with whom she was so secretly yet gloriously one.

After the birth of Jesus, the unspoken heart-to-heart oneness, the communing, doubtless continued as it has for thousands of other mothers who have held their babies to their breasts, felt them guzzling, stroked their downy heads, marvelled at their well-formed fingers and their perfect toes, watched and loved them with an adoring, wordless love. Even when Jesus was weaned, though he was no longer dependent on her in the same way, through shared mother–son experiences, Mary's connectedness with Jesus continued: as she taught him to pray, as they gazed at the stars together, as they marvelled at the wild flowers that studded the meadows in the spring, as they mixed yeast with flour and watched the dough rise.

The result of this intimacy was a bonding between them that was both beautiful and unbreakable even though their relationship was subjected to a series of radical changes.

The complete communion they enjoyed when Mary carried Jesus in her womb gave way to the partial communion of the pre-weaned infant and his mother. This phase, in turn, was resolved into the separateness every mother has to come to terms with when her baby becomes autonomous – still part of her, yet a little person in his own right.

Yet another change occurred when Jesus reached the age of maturity – two years after his first visit to the temple where he declared his life goal: 'I must be about my Father's business . . .' (Luke 2:49). Doubtless they still enjoyed intimacy with one another, particularly on the Sabbath when, like other Jewish families, they celebrated the Passover together; but the oneness was now being expressed very differently from Jesus' pre-natal or pre-weaned days.

Yet another change occurred in their relationship in Jesus' eighteenth year. The rabbis insisted that, by the age of eighteen, a young man should be married. To be fruitful and multiply was God's design for the whole of creation. Anyone who strayed from this plan threatened God's world order. While many questioned and criticised Jesus' singleness, Mary and Jesus shared their silent secret – his origins, his real fatherhood, his destiny, his mission, the real reason for his celibacy. Such secrets bind together those who share them.

Physical absence

Eventually and inevitably, the day dawned when Mary knew that she stood on the brink of yet another transition in her relationship with her God-Son. Rumours reached them that John the Baptist had emerged from the desert – to pave the way for Jesus' public ministry. Jesus could not have left the home in Nazareth with integrity unless Mary gave him her blessing.[13] Did Mary struggle to say her 'yes' to the pain of the physical separation after so many years of togetherness or, like Abraham, was she ready to entrust her Son to God's keeping? We are not told. Neither are we told what happened to her as she remained in the hiddenness of Nazareth. We may safely assume, however, that she remains in Nazareth with a host of happy memories, the awareness that Jesus is still her Son, that ongoing sense of oneness that spans rivers and mountain ranges – yet with his empty chair, that symbol of real, acutely felt absence. The absence of her Beloved.

During his prolonged absence, her faith does not fail her. It burns bright within her breast. So much so that, when Jesus returns and accompanies her to the wedding in Cana, their communing continues. When a catering crisis threatens the reputation of the bride's parents, therefore, they both know that Jesus has the ability to rescue the situation by performing a miracle. Mary, it must be remembered, was not a sophisticated twentieth-century Western woman schooled in psychological insights. She was a Middle Eastern mother and here she behaves like one – assuming that, even though her Son is now an adult, he still needs her guidance and wisdom, direction and encouragement. 'The time has come to unleash your miraculous powers,' she implies. Despite the cultural context, Jesus responds with a resounding 'No! . . . It's no longer *your* right, Mother. We must let God be God. Let him decide. I have come to do *his* will.'

Jesus had been subject to his mother all his life. Does his resolve sound like a rebuke? If so, does it wound her? Does it remind her of that occasion when, as a twelve-year-old, Jesus had asked: 'Didn't you know I had to be in my Father's house?' (Luke 2:49)? Possibly. Yet it seems probable that she was the only wedding guest who was not surprised when Jesus 'revealed his glory' by changing jugs of water into jugs of vintage wine (John 2:11). Such is her faith in him.

The search
After the wedding, Jesus leaves her again. Like any Middle

Eastern mother, she pines for her Son. She goes searching for him. She finds him. Does she go only with the intention of questioning his sanity and attempting to rescue him from the punishing schedule that prevents him from eating properly (Mark 3:21)? Or does she go partly because life without him feels unbearable? Does devotion to him prompt her to pursue him? Is she like the lover in the Song of Songs – languishing for the physical closeness of her Beloved? The Gospel writers only underline the former. They also emphasise that, once again, Jesus wounds her. Once again, this is the wounding of deep, committed love. He wants her to act in a way that runs counter to their culture – to free him to do God's will. To her credit, she appears to master this difficult task. Surely, that is one reason why, on Good Friday, she stands at the foot of the Cross utterly helpless. As she gazes at her Son who is suffering such a cruel, pain-filled, lingering death, we witness the dramatic change that has come over her. Here she attempts less and less leaving her Son to achieve more and more. All she can do in that agonising moment is to stand by and watch – helplessly, hopelessly. But Jesus, even though he is at the point of death, suffers no such handicap. Just before he breathes his last breath, he gives her what she most needs – a friend and mentor; his best friend, John.

Mary now enters the desert of absence *par excellence*. His death. Does she cope with it by clinging to the belief that, just as he promised, he would return? Possibly. She is a woman of great faith and, as John of the Cross reminds us, 'Faith tells us of things we have never seen, and cannot come to know by our natural senses.'[14] And, of course, Jesus did return. He returned to Jerusalem. He returned to Mary. He returned to the disciples.

A new challenge now faces Mary – to negotiate the relationship on yet another new set of terms. Her Beloved is clearly the same yet curiously different. She is still his mother but their relationship has changed yet again. As she continues to

commune with him and with her own heart, does she hear him say what he said to Mary Magdalene: 'Don't cling. Don't cling to me as I was, accept me as I am. Don't cling to our relationship as it was, precious though it was. Be ready to move on into a renewed relationship with me. I want to be as intimate as ever but I am Other.' Such scene-shifts in relationships are not easy to negotiate but Jesus loved his mother and wanted to wean her away from a dependency on his felt presence before that impending bitter-sweet moment of parting that was to come on Ascension Day. Mary continues to learn the difficult lessons of her Son's absence – that lack of immediacy does not equal lack of oneness or lack of care. She continues to discover that, in her relationship with her God-Son, she can no longer depend on seeing him face to face, on feeling his arms embrace her, on experiencing the energising at-oneness she enjoyed before his Crucifixion. Now, she must endure his real absence and learn to touch and hold and see and sense him only with the comparative barrenness of faith.

She learns these lessons with dignity and courage. That is why, between Ascension Day and the Day of Pentecost, we find her humbly enjoying fellowship with other believers (Acts 1:14). Her relationship with her Son now goes through yet another metamorphosis as she sits and waits in the city for the Spirit's empowering.

While she waits, does it become even more clear to her that now the initiative in the relationship lies solely with Jesus? The timing of their encounters is his. When he has something to say, he will speak. When he wants to bring healing to someone, so long as she remains open to be a channel through which his power can flow, he will use her, speak through her, love through

---

Mary was familiar with the desert of absence.

her. Even though, at times, her senses may seem numb so that she can no longer see him or sense him, feel him or encounter him, he is there as he promised when he said: 'Never will I leave you; never will I forsake you' (Hebrews 13:5).

In chapter one, I mentioned Hannah Hurnard's charming allegorical tale, *Hind's Feet in High Places*, where the heroine, Much-Afraid was taken into the desert by the Chief Shepherd she served. The desert so transforms Much-Afraid that the Chief Shepherd gives her a new name: Acceptance-With-Joy. Reminiscing on her desert wanderings, Acceptance-With-Joy recalls:

> I learnt that I must ACCEPT WITH JOY all that You allowed to happen to me on the way and everything to which the path led me! That I was never to evade it but to accept it and lay down my own will on the altar and say: 'Behold me, I am Thy little handmaiden, Acceptance-With-Joy.'[15]

Just as Acceptance-With-Joy echoes the 'Yes' that Mary uttered so willingly when the angel announced that she had been chosen to become the mother of the Messiah, so Mary fleshes out Acceptance-With-Joy's determination. As Acceptance-With-Joy put it on another occasion: 'I MUST love You as long as I continue to exist. I cannot live without loving You.'[16]

In other words, the Mary who waits for the empowering of the Spirit is a very different Mary from the teenager who whispered her first momentous 'Yes' to God.

The mature Mary has learned that one such yes must give birth to a succession of smaller but no less painful yesses. The mature Mary is even more full of grace than on that day when the heavenly Father chose her to be the mother of his Son. The desert of absence stripped her of her motherly possessiveness. She now seems to be content to love and serve him from afar. Full of faith and poise, she is, indeed, 'the most blessed of women' because her life still revolves around him in love. Like the Lover in the Song of Songs, she can sing with integrity, 'My Beloved is mine and I am his. The banner he raises over me is love – love no flood can quench, no torrents drown. Under his eyes I have found true peace.'[17] The awareness of such never-ending love has been the desert's gift to her. God intends that it should be the desert's gift to us also – for the desert is a place of promise that gives birth to worship.

Often, it is in looking back that such worship is born. That is why I suggest we close this chapter with a time of reflection asking:

- Have I ever enjoyed intimacy with God? When was that?
- When feelings of heart-to-heart closeness with God evaporate, what do I do? How do I feel? Can I trust that such times deepen my longing for God?
- Have I learned to do less and less so that God can achieve more and more?
- Have I learned to allow God to take the initiative in my relationship with him?
- Have I ever said a 'Yes' to God that gave birth to a string of other 'yesses'? When was that? What happened as a result?

Journeying through the desert.

Songs in the Desert

The desert is a place of stripping and a place of terror, a place of wonder and a place of promise, a place of testing and a place of paralysis of the soul. The desert, as we have observed throughout this book, may be a situation of helplessness and hopelessness, a state of mental anguish, deep-down loneliness or emotional emptiness. The desert, alternatively, can be a place where God whispers words of tenderness right into our hearts, a place where we meet with our Creator in a life-changing way. The desert often proves to be the place where our relationship with God deepens, where we encounter him in never-to-be-forgotten ways.

When we linger in the physical desert, our awareness of our external surroundings is sharpened, the ears of our heart become attuned to the powerful language of creation, our internal dialogue gradually dies down and our hearts open like a flower in summer. This sharpening of the senses and this heart openness prompts desert dwellers to record their responses to the God of the desert. Such responses, when read slowly and meditatively, with the mind and the heart, the intellect and the imagination, can thrill us and trigger praise, worship and adoration. That is why this book began with two jubilant desert songs and ends on a similar crescendo with some of the magnificent paeons of praise that have soared from desert places or those who have suffered desert-like emotions. Allow the images to become imprinted on your mind and heart. Open yourself afresh to see and hear and sense and know God. Enjoy a fresh encounter with this living, loving Lord of the desert.

The Desert – A Place of Worship

O LORD my God, you are very great;
  you are clothed with splendour and majesty.
He wraps himself in light as with a garment;
  he stretches out the heavens like a tent
  and lays the beams of his upper chambers on their waters.
He makes the clouds his chariot
  and rides on the wings of the wind.
He makes winds his messengers,
  flames of fire his servants.

He set the earth on its foundations;
  it can never be moved.
You covered it with the deep as with a garment;
  the waters stood above the mountains.
But at your rebuke the waters fled,
  at the sound of your thunder they took to flight;
they flowed over the mountains,
  they went down into the valleys,
  to the place you assigned for them.
You set a boundary they cannot cross;
  never again will they cover the earth.

He makes springs pour water into the ravines;
  it flows between the mountains.
They give water to all the beasts of the field;
  the wild donkeys quench their thirst.
The birds of the air nest by the waters;
  they sing among the branches.
He waters the mountains from his upper chambers;
  the earth is satisfied by the fruit of his work.

(Psalm 104:1-13)

Ascribe to the LORD, O mighty ones,
    ascribe to the LORD, glory and strength.
Ascribe to the LORD the glory due to his name;
    worship the LORD in the splendour of his holiness

The voice of the LORD is over the waters;
    the God of glory thunders,
    the LORD thunders over the mighty waters.
The voice of the LORD is powerful;
    the voice of the LORD is majestic . . .
The voice of the LORD strikes
    with flashes of lightning.
The voice of the LORD shakes the desert.

(Psalm 29:1–9)

Come, let's shout praises to Yahweh,
    raise the roof for the Rock who saved us!
Let's march into his presence singing praises,
    lifting the rafters with our hymns!

And why? Because Yahweh is the best,
    High King over all the gods.
In one hand he holds deep caves and caverns,
    in the other hand grasps the high mountains.
He made Ocean – and he owns it!
    His hands sculpted Earth!

So come, let us worship; bow before him,
    on your knees before Yahweh who made us!
Oh yes, he's our God,
    and we're the people he pastures, the flock he feeds.

(Psalm 95; The Message)

A Song of Moses

I will proclaim the name of the LORD,
    Oh, praise the greatness of our God!
He is the Rock, his works are perfect,
    and all his ways are just.
A faithful God who does no wrong,
    upright and just is he . . .
In a desert land he found him,
    in a barren and howling waste.
He shielded him and cared for him;
    he guarded him as the apple of his eye,
like an eagle that stirs up its nest
    and hovers over its young,
that spreads its wings to catch them
    and carries them on its pinions.
The LORD alone led him;
    no foreign god was with him.

(Deuteronomy 32:3,4,10–12)

A Song of Mary

(sung in the desert of rejection by Joseph)

'I'm bursting with God-news;
I'm dancing the song of my Saviour God.
God took one good look at me, and look what happened –
I'm the most fortunate woman on earth!
What God has done for me will never be forgotten,
The God whose very name is holy, set apart from all others.
His mercy flows in wave after wave
On those who are in awe before him.

(Luke 1:46–50; The Message)

A Song of John

(penned in the desert of exile)

Glory and strength to Christ, who loves us,
who blood-washed our sins from our lives.
Who made us a Kingdom, Priests for his Father,
forever – and yes, he's on his way!
Riding the clouds, he'll be seen by every eye,
Those who mocked and killed him will see him . . .
Oh, Yes.

(Revelation 1:5–7; The Message)

The Desert – A Place of Wonder

Isaiah's Song

'To whom will you compare me?
    Or who is my equal?' says the Holy One.
Lift your eyes and look to the heavens.
    Who created all these?
Who brings out the starry host one by one,
    and calls them each by name.
Because of his great power and mighty strength,
    not one of them is missing.

(Isaiah 40:25–26)

God's Song

(sung to Job in the desert of his distress)

Have you ever given orders to the morning,
    or shown the dawn its place . . .
Have you journeyed to the springs of the sea

or walked in the recesses of the deep?. . .
Have you comprehended the vast expanses of the earth? . . .
What is the way to the abode of light?
And where does darkness reside? . . .
Have you entered the storehouses of the snow
    or seen the storehouses of the hail? . . .

                      (Job 38:12 ff)

The Desert – A Place of Promise

The desert and the parched land will be glad;
    the wilderness will rejoice and blossom.
Like the crocus, it will burst into bloom;
    it will rejoice greatly and shout for joy.

I will put in the desert
    the cedar and the acacia, the myrtle and the olive.
I will set pines in the wasteland,
    the fir and the cypress together,
so that people may see and know,
    may consider and understand,
that the hand of the LORD has done this,
    that the Holy One of Israel has created it.

                 (Isaiah 41:17–20)

Jesus' Promise
(given to John in the desert of exile)

'See, I come quickly! I carry My reward with me, and repay
everyone according to his deeds. I am Alpha and Omega, the

First and the Last, the Beginning and the End. Happy are those
who wash their robes, for they have the right to the Tree of Life
and the freedom of the gates of the City . . .'
The Spirit and the Bride say, 'Come!'. . .
Let the thirsty come, and let everyone who wishes take the Water
of Life as a gift . . .
'Yes, I am coming very quickly'
'Amen, come, Lord Jesus!'

(Revelation 22:12,17ff JB)

Notes

INTRODUCTION
1. Revelation 22:17 and a flashback to verse 1.
2. I am indebted to Professor James Houston of Regent College, Vancouver for the insight that the Bible starts with a garden, ends with a city and majors on the desert wanderings that sandwich the two.
3. Eugene Peterson's paraphrase of Psalm 8 taken from *The Message: The Psalms* (Colorado Springs, NavPress, 1994) p 13.

CHAPTER ONE
1. Eugene Peterson's paraphrase from *The Message* (Colorado Springs, NavPress, 1993).
2. That's why Satan could tempt him to turn stones into bread. He wouldn't tempt us in that way because he knows and we know that we couldn't do it.
3. Mark, it must be remembered, can have heard of this story only from Jesus himself.
4. Here I am indebted to William Barclay's description of the Judean desert in *The Gospel of Saint Matthew* (Edinburgh, St Andrew Press, 1994) p.63.
5. Michael Green's phrase.
6. Michael Green, *I Believe in Satan's Downfall* (London, Hodder and Stoughton, 1984) p 48.
7. Michael Green's insights culled from ibid. p 50.
8. Eugene Peterson's paraphrase of Matthew 4:10, op. cit.
9. Sister Margaret Magdalene CSMV *Jesus Man of Prayer* (Guildford, Eagle, 1998) p.41.
10. Ibid. p.42.
11. Sister Margaret Magdalene's phrase.
12. Eugene Peterson's paraphrase from *The Message*, op. cit.
13. My adaptation of Hymns of Good Friday, Orthodox Liturgy.
14. Mattins for Holy Saturday, Orthodox Liturgy.
15. William Barclay, *The Gospel of Jesus* (Edinburgh, St Andrew Press, 1994) p 64.
16. Sister Margaret Magdalene CSMV, *Jesus Man of Prayer*, op. cit. , pp 39,40.
17. Hannah Hurnard, *Hind's Feet on High Places* (Olive Press, 1966) p 54.

CHAPTER TWO
1. Quoted William Barclay, *The Letter to the Hebrews* (Edinburgh, St Andrew Press, 1994) p 143.

2. Maria Boulding, *The Coming of God* (London, SPCK, 1982) pp 1, 7–8.
3. See Joshua 24:2.
4. Carlo Carretto, *Letters from the Desert* (London, DLT, 1976) pp 137–138
5. See Genesis 11:32 where, as soon as Terah dies, Abram resumes the pilgrimage
6. James Houston's phrase. I'm drawing here on his insights explained in a talk on the desert given to students at Schloss Mittersill, Austria.
7. Quoted in John Michael Talbot, *The Lover and the Beloved* (London, Marshall Pickering, 1987) pp 4,6.
8. Thomas Green SJ, *Drinking From a Dry Well* (Ave Maria Press, 1991) p 20.
9. Ibid. p 20.
10. Eugene Peterson, paraphrase of part of Psalm 121 taken from *The Message: The Psalms* (Colorado Springs, NavPress, 1994), p13.

CHAPTER THREE
1. Moshe Pearlman, *In the Footsteps of Moses* (Nateeve Publishing 1976) p 9.
2. Numbers 12:3.
3. Moshe Pearlman, op. cit. p 9.
4. Ibid. p 96.
5. Carlo Carretto, *In Search of the Beyond* (London, DLT 1975) p 23.
6. David Runcorn, *Space for God* (London, DLT Daybreak 1990) p 121.
7. Ibid. p 121.
8. See, for example, Exodus 5:22,23.
9. Sue Monk Kidd, *When the Heart Waits* (Harper and Row 1990) p 22.
10. Antoine St Exupery, *The Little Prince* (Piccolo Books 1983) p 75.
11. Karen Manton, 'Unpublished Journal'. Quoted in *Rivers in the Desert.* (Albatross, 1991) p 75.
12. Revised English Bible. Quoted in *Rivers in the Desert* op. cit. p 108.

CHAPTER FOUR
1. Deuteronomy 34:10,12 JB and GNB.
2. Lance Pierson, *Standing for God in a Hostile World* (Leicester, IVP, 1989) pp 18–19.
3. Albert Osborn, 'The Silences of Christ'. Quoted in *Rivers in the Desert*, ed. Rowland Croucher (Albatross Books, 1991) p 15.
4. See also Hosea 2:5,8.
5. David Runcorn, *Space for God* (London, DLT, Daybreak, 1990) p 53.
6. Andre Louf, *Teach Us to Pray*. Trans. Hubert Hoskins (London, DLT, 1974) p 70.
7. Lance Pierson op. cit. p 50.

8.   Ibid. p 37.
9.   1 Kings 19:10,14.
10. James Houston
11. Lance Pierson's phrase.
12. John A. Sanford, *Ministry Burnout* (London, Arthur James Ltd, 1982) p 12.
13. I am continuing to draw on John Sanford's insights on burnout here.
14. James Houston ibid.
15. Lance Pierson's phrase.
16. Marjorie Foyle's phrase from the title of her book *Honourably Wounded* (London, MARC, Monarch, Interserve and EMA, 1987)
17. The quotation in double quotes is from 1 Kings 19:18.
18. James Houston, *The Hungry Soul* (Oxford, Lion Publishing, 1992) pp 186–187.

CHAPTER FIVE

1.   Jocelyn Murray, *Windows on Widowhood* (Godalming, Highland Books, 1995) p 22.
2.   A room rather like the one made available to Elisha in 2 Kings 4:10.
3.   Joyce Rupp, *Praying Our Goodbyes* (Guildford, Eagle 1995) p 104.
4.   Joyce Rupp commenting on Victor Frankl's claim in ibid. p 43.
5.   See also Genesis 20.
6.   A hermit in a personal letter to me.
7.   James Houston, *The Hungry Soul* (Oxford, Lion Publishing, 1992) pp 187–188.
8.   Moshe Pearlman, *In the Footsteps of Moses* (Oliphants, 1976) p 31.
9.   Maria Boulding commenting on Ex. 12:21–23; 29–32 in *Gateway to Hope: An Exploration of Failure* (London, Fount Paperbacks, 1985) p 22.
10. Maria Boulding, op. cit. p.25.
11. Leslie F. Brandt, *A Book of Christian Prayers*. Quoted in *Rivers in the Desert* (Albatross, 1991).
12. Maria Boulding, op. cit. p 30.
13. Jesus' own story of the prodigal son prompts me to make this claim. No son worthy of the name would leave the parental home without the parents' blessing.
14. John of the Cross, *The Ascent of Mount Carmel*, quoted in *Lamps of Fire*, edited by Elizabeth Ruth ODC (DLT, 1995) p 1.
15. Hannah Hurnard, *Hind's Feet on High Places* (Olive Press, 1966) p 148.
16. Ibid. p 105.
17. The Song of Songs 2:13, 2:4, 4:6 and 4:10 JB.

THE EXPLORING PRAYER SERIES

Edited by Joyce Huggett

This series helps point the reader to God by drawing on the authors' own extensive church and life experiences.

Joyce Huggett
HEARING JESUS
0 86348 304 0
A fresh look at the parables of *The Sower* and *The Good Samaritan* through a historical and cultural context.

Joan Hutson
HEAL MY HEART O LORD
0 86347 213 3
Prayers and poems written for the broken-hearted, accompanied by sensitive line-drawings and watercolours.

Wendy Miller
SPIRITUAL FRIENDSHIP
0 86347 129 3
Reflecting on her own prayer pilgrimage the author shows how to building relationships through prayer and meditation.

Michael Mitton
THE SOUNDS OF GOD
0 86347 067 X
Examining how various strands of spirituality, from charismatics to contemplatives, hear the voice of God.

Gerald O'Mahony
FINDING THE STILL POINT
0 86347 110 2
Help in understanding and governing mood swings and looking for the 'still' point where we can find God.

Joyce Rupp
PRAYING OUR GOODBYES
0 86347 154 4
A helpful book about coping with goodbyes, whether to a partner, a job, a home or a friend.